Twayne's English Authors Series

EDITOR OF THIS VOLUME

Arthur F. Kinney

University of Massachusetts at Amherst

Joseph Hall

TEAS 250

Joseph Hall

JOSEPH HALL /

By LEONARD D. TOURNEY ·

University of Tulsa

TWAYNE PUBLISHERS

A DIVISION OF G. K. HALL & CO., BOSTON

Copyright © 1979 by G. K. Hall & Co.

Published in 1979 by Twayne Publishers,
A Division of G. K. Hall & Co.
All Rights Reserved

Printed on permanent/durable acid-free paper and bound
in the United States of America

First Printing

Library of Congress Cataloging in Publication Data

Tourney, Leonard D
    Joseph Hall.

(Twayne's English authors series ; TEAS 250)
Bibliography: p. 149–51
Includes index.
1. Hall, Joseph, Bp. of Norwich, 1574–1656—
Criticism and interpretation.
PR2283. H7Z88 1979   828 '.3 '09   78-12648
ISBN 0-8057-6740-1

79127

Contents

About the Author

Leonard D. Tourney received his Ph.D. from the University of California, Santa Barbara, in 1972. Now Associate Professor of English at the University of Tulsa, he has published articles on seventeenth-century English Literature in such journals as *Studies in Philology*, *Papers on Language & Literature*, and *Essays in Literature*.

Preface

In the England of Charles I, Joseph Hall was an important public figure, revered as a bishop and admired for his piety, learning, and moderation. His moral treatises were translated and imitated; his polemics, vigorous defenses of the Church of England against Papist and Puritan, became focal points of controversy. Yet his life had tragic features. From the heights of episcopal dignity he plummeted into a dangerous obscurity when Charles fell to Cromwell and a new ecclesiastical order prevailed, but what he once referred to as his "hard measure"—arrest, imprisonment, sequestration—he bore with Stoic hardihood. He did not live to experience what to men of letters is that hardest measure of all, the loss of readers. The eighteenth century admired the polish of his verse satires; the nineteenth his religious works as an impressive number of new editions during that period attested. Sadly, in more recent years Hall's writings have become the preserve of scholars and antiquaries.

But Hall deserves more than antiquarian interest. As a youthful satirist he stimulated, if not initiated, a vogue for Juvenalian verse satire in the late 1590's; as a moralist, he introduced at least two prose genres into the seventeenth-century literary scene, the "epistle," and the "character." And as a priest and bishop his meditations, sermons, commentaries, and polemics place him with John Donne, Lancelot Andrewes, and Jeremy Taylor in a distinguished company of Anglican divines who made the language of religious devotion luminous and the prose of their century distinguished. For Hall was more than a prolific author; he was a conscious stylist. With Montaigne, Bacon, and Jonson, Hall helped shape the contours of modern prose; and like the works of his greater contemporaries, Hall's index the preoccupations of the seventeenth-century mind—its intellectual ardor, religious passion, and acute sense of marking both the beginning and the end of an epoch.

In writing about Hall, I have tried to avoid the temptation of making him seem a greater man, author, or influence than he was. He was a minor figure, and so he should remain. But I have also tried not to undervalue Hall, for such I believe has been his usual fate in the hands of moderns. His nineteenth-century biographers, clergymen themselves, were primarily interested in his spiritual attainments and church preferments. The picture of Hall they present is that of a pious bishop who was also incidentally, and perhaps unfortunately, a man of letters. Twentieth century criticism has presented an equally fragmented view of Hall: as a satirist, a moralist, or controversialist who was incidentally a bishop. But Hall's literary career, like that of any author's, equals more than the sum of its parts. In this study I attempt to emphasize the coherence and artistry of his achievement by making his literary and intellectual premises plain, by defining the distinctive features of his style, and by relating his ideas to those of his time. The plan of the book is generic and chronological. I treat first Hall's life, then, in order, his satires, moral treatises, poems, meditations, sermons, and polemics. Such an ordering demonstrates both the progress and variety of his efforts as an author. A brief concluding chapter takes up the significance of Hall's work and particularly the controversial matter of his originality. Because Hall was a prolific writer, I have with one exception restricted my attention to his English works and those which best exemplify the spirit and design of his authorship.

For Hall's poetry, I have used Arnold Davenport's excellent edition of the *Collected Poems,* accommodating the modern reader with minor changes in spelling and punctuation. For the prose, I have used the Wynter edition. Although Wynter is not completely trustworthy, it is the most nearly so and is readily available in several modern reprints. Quotations from Hall's Latin authors are regularly from the Loeb Library editions.

Part of Chapter 4 appeared earlier in a somewhat different version in an article published in *Papers on Language & Literature;* I am grateful to the editors of that journal for permission to use previously published material. I would also like to thank the Director and staff of the Henry E. Huntington Library and Art Gallery for permission to examine early editions of Hall's works; the reference librarians of the McFarlin Library, University of Tulsa, for their unfailing assistance in obtaining books; and the Research Office of the same institution for a generous financial grant. Professors Frank L. Huntley of the University of Michigan and Gerhard Müller-Schwefe of the University of Tübingen provided me with useful information, offprints, and encouragement. My greatest debt, as always, is to my wife and children.

LEONARD D. TOURNEY

The University of Tulsa

Chronology

1574   Joseph Hall born 1 July, parish of Ashby-de-la-Zouch, Leicestershire.

1589   Begins academic career at Emmanuel College, Cambridge (Bachelor of Arts, 1592/3; Master of Arts, 1596; Bachelor of Divinity, 1603; Doctor of Divinity, 1610).

1597   First three books of *Virgidemiae* published anonymously.

1598   Second three books ("The Biting Satires") of *Virgidemiae* published with Hall named as author.

1600   Ordained at Colchester, 14 December.

1601   Leaves Cambridge to become rector of Hawstead in Suffolk.

1603   Death of Elizabeth I. Hall marries Elizabeth Winniff, and publishes *The Kings Prophecie*, a poem in tribute to James I.

1605   *Meditations and Vowes Divine and Moral* and *Mundus Alter et Idem*. Accompanies Sir Edmund Bacon to the Netherlands, where Hall composes a second century of *Meditations*.

1606   *The Art of Divine Meditation* and *Heaven Upon Earth*.

1607   Leaves Hawstead to become rector at Waltham Holy Cross, Essex. Publishes *Holy Observations*.

1608   Appointed chaplain to Prince Henry's *Characters of Vertues and Vices* and two volumes of *Epistles* also published.

1609   *The Peace of Rome*. John Healey's translation of Hall's *Mundus Alter et Idem* published as *The Discovery of a New World*.

1612   Death of Prince Henry. Hall publishes first volume of *Contemplations Upon the Principal Passages of the Holy Story* (second volume published in 1614).

1613   Contributes three sets of verses to Joshua Sylvester's *Lachrymae Lachrymarum* (third edition), a collection of funeral elegies on the death of Prince Henry. Writes prefatory poems to Donne's *Anniversaries*.

1616   Travels to France as chaplain to Viscount Doncaster, English Ambassador to French court. Becomes Dean of Worcester while continuing to serve congregation at Waltham.

1617   Attends King James to the Perth Conference in Scotland.

1618   Serves as delegate to Synod of Dort in Holland.

1624   Refuses Bishopric of Gloucester.

1625   Death of James I.

1627   Consecrated Bishop of Exeter 23 December.

1630   *Occasional Meditations.*

1640   *Episcopacy by Divine Right.* Smectymnuan controversy. For the next two years Hall exchanges polemics with Presbyterians and John Milton.

1641   Translated to the bishopric of Norwich. On 30 December Hall, Archbishop Williams, and eleven other bishops arrested and sent to the Tower of London charged with high treason.

1642   Hall released from the Tower; takes up his duties at Norwich.

1643   In April Parliament passes the Ordinance of Sequestration; Hall deprived of his bishopric and episcopal revenues impounded.

1648   Ejected from episcopal residence at Norwich; moves with his family to a small house in Higham, several miles north of the city. *Breathings of the Devout Soul.*

1650   *Susurrium Cum Deo.*

1651   *The Invisible World Discovered to Spiritual Eyes.*

1656   Dies 8 September; buried in the parish churchyard at Higham.

CHAPTER 1

Quill and Crosier

O F an age when a man's social origins were fair game for an opponent's scorn, the satirist John Marston labelled Joseph Hall a "swineherd's brat."[1] In fact, Hall's beginnings were not that humble, although his father may have risen to his office as bailiff of the Earl of Huntingdon from a more menial capacity. In any case, if not born to the gentry, young Hall at least found parents who could feed and clothe him properly, see to his education, and furnish him with motives to rise in the world. Hall's progress from bailiff's son to bishop was the stuff his contemporary Thomas Deloney might have shaped into an Elizabethan success story.

I *Early Years*

Hall was born 1 July 1574, in the parish of Ashby-de-la-Zouch, Leicestershire. His mother Winifride was a woman of austere piety whose days, Hall later recalled, were given to "private devotion" and "undissembled mortification."[2] Her spiritual mentor, Antony Gilby, vicar of Ashby, was author of several virulent anti-Roman tracts and may have played spiritual mentor to Hall as well, as in a less direct way did the Earl of Huntingdon, who was well known for his Puritan sympathies.[3] Such influences gave Hall's life a certain direction and tone. The Puritanism of his youth accounted for the chief elements of his character—moral sobriety, intellectual certitude, and a conviction of God's Providence he would later acknowledge with characteristic modesty: "What I have done is worthy nothing but silence and forgetfulness; but what God hath done for me is worthy everlasting and thankful memory."[4]

Hall was a younger son; that, family influence, and his own religious nature lighted his steps to a life in the Church, then precariously situated on the Elizabethan compromise. Of his first instruction Hall gives no account. That it was at Ashby and under Anto

Gilby is likely enough, and if his earliest schooling was in any way typical, it consisted largely of ponderous helpings of Latin grammar, some Greek, and much translation and imitation of ancient authors, chiefly Cicero.[5] The end of his labors was such learning deemed necessary to an Elizabethan clergyman to preach, to write, and to read learned commentaries and polemics. But his studies also opened to Hall horizons much broader than those of rural Leicestershire. The England of Hall's youth was a world of contradictions: regal majesty kept company with incredible squalor, medieval credulity with Renaissance aspiration, classical scholarship and Christian idealism with economic exploitation, cruel and short shrift for heretics, and crass materialism. All this, and Gilby's anti-Papist anecdotes, Hall must have absorbed with his Cicero, and interpreted all in the light of his developing religious bias, which looked to the Scriptures for wisdom, to Geneva and Germany for their interpretation, and practiced forms of worship stripped of the Popish idolatry and superstition Hall learned early to detest.[6] His education was thus more than a curriculum. It was participation in what one chronicler of the period has called "the most intense and electric experience of a young people coming to maturity, with new worlds opening out before them, not only across the seas but in the mind."[7]

Hall was a bright pupil and his academic talents were quickly recognized. When Ashby's school had given Hall all it could, his father considered committing him to a private tutor who might equip him for his vocation at less expense. But Abraham, Joseph's brother, protested, determined not to see Joseph's talents wasted in a small, provincial market town. Hall's father gave in, and in 1589, at the age of fifteen, Joseph Hall matriculated in Emmanuel College, Cambridge.

Emmanuel was the strictest of Cambridge colleges. Founded in 1584 by Sir Walter Mildmay, its express mission was the training of a learned and articulate clergy of the Puritan persuasion.[8] As in all educational institutions of the age, logic, rhetoric, and grammar— the medieval "trivium"—formed the core of instruction, supplemented by the work of modern Humanists such as Vives, Ramus, and Sturm. But at Emmanuel College, especially, Calvinist theology with its uncompromising doctrine of predestination and its missionary zeal dominated the curriculum. Public lectures, polemical sermons, and the counsel of his tutor, Nathanael Gilby, son of

Ashby's Puritan vicar, reinforced the personal piety and intellectual discipline which were to remain the larger features of Hall's personality, even after his Puritan zeal had resolved itself into Anglican moderation.

Although Hall distinguished himself as a scholar, his academic career was plagued by financial problems. In his third year of residence it appeared he would have to leave Cambridge until an uncle volunteered to underwrite half the cost of his expenses. Later, following his graduation as Bachelor of Arts in 1592/3 and through the influence of the Earl of Huntingdon, Hall became a Fellow of the college, thereby securing his maintenance. In 1596 he proceeded Master of Arts, and on 14 December 1600, he took Holy Orders, thus culminating his long spiritual apprenticeship.

Man and boy, Hall spent nearly thirteen years at Cambridge. During his later residency he engaged often in public disputations, held the University Lectureship in Rhetoric for two years, and following his ordination, preached often both in the university and in the neighboring towns.[9] During the same period he commenced authorship. His first efforts, by his own accounts, were pastoral poems now lost.[10] He may have composed lines for some of the Parnassus Plays. More important were his *Virgidemiae*, caustic verses by which he established a reputation as a satirist in 1597. By the year of the second edition, 1599, Hall's satires narrowly escaped the fate of others of their kind when a number of works damned as scurrilous by the authorities were committed to the flames in London. At the last moment, Hall's satires were reprieved, and although he ventured again as a satirist in a Latin prose fiction, *Mundus Alter et Idem*, several years later, this was to be published anonymously and was to carry the imprint of Frankfort, although as Arnold Davenport has suggested it was probably printed in London.[11]

II *Ecclesiastical Honors*

For all their rigor, Hall considered his days at Cambridge the happiest of his life. Yet although his academic career had been distinguished, he never intended it to be permanent, and following his ordination he began to seek employment in the calling for which he had so long prepared. In 1601, invited to become headmaster of a newly founded school in Devonshire, Hall traveled to London with Dr. Lawrence Chaderton, Master of Emmanuel, to be interviewed by Chief Justice Popam for the post. Popam found Hall's manner and education more than satisfactory, and made an offer. It was an attractive one; good livings were then scarce and Hall's duties would have been largely administrative. It was not, however, what he had envisioned for himself; and although he accepted the offer, he had no sooner left the presence of the Chief Justice than he received a letter from Lady Anne Drury, wife of Sir Robert Drury of Suffolk, offering him the rectorship at Hawstead. "Methinks," Hall told Dr. Chaderton, "God pulls me by the sleeve and tells me it is his will I should rather go to the east than to the west."[12] Hall promptly returned to his first benefactor, recommended a Cambridge roommate in his place, and wrote to Lady Drury accepting her offer. He was instituted as rector of Hawstead 2 December 1601.

In Sir Robert and Lady Anne Drury, Hall found distinguished and well-connected patrons. Anne Bacon was a niece of Sir Francis and daughter of Sir Nicholas Bacon.[13] Her husband, a soldier of a family of soldiers, had been knighted at the age of sixteen, had served both on the Continent and in Ireland, and at the time of Hall's appointment owned extensive properties in Suffolk and London. Hall's relations with Lady Drury were cordial; those with her energetic and irascible husband less so, largely, according to Hall, because of a certain Mr. Lilly, characterized by Hall as a "witty and bold atheist" who had prejudiced his patron's mind against the young cleric. Lilly's influence, however, was short-lived. He died of the plague within a few months of Hall's installation, and thereafter Hall's relations with Drury improved. In a long poem, "The Kings Prophecie" composed on the occasion of King James' succession in 1603, Hall hailed his patron in language that suggests the two men had reconciled their differences:

> And thou, renowned Drury mongst the rest,
> Above the rest, whether thee still detain
> The snowy Alps, or if thou thought it best
> To trust thy speed unto the watery plain
> Shalt him receive; he thee, with such sweet grace
> As may beseem thy worth and noble race.[14]

Hall married at Hawstead, began a family, and won increasing reputation as a preacher and author.[15] Responding to what he saw as a lack of practical guides to Christian (Protestant) meditation, he wrote a series of small volumes exemplifying such meditation and expressing the Christian Stoicism that would later win for him the title "The English Seneca": *Meditations and Vowes* (1605), *Heaven Upon Earth* (1606), and *The Art of Divine Meditation* (1606). To these same years belong his *Epistles* (two volumes, 1606; 1608), a collection of essays on diverse themes, and his *Characters of Vertues and Vices,* an attempt to imitate the Theophrastan "character." In these last two endeavors, Hall was a pioneer, for neither the charac ter nor the epistle had previously been written in England.

If R. C. Bald is correct in identifying the "Mr. Lilly" of Hall's memoir as William Lyly, husband of John Donne's sister Anne, then Hall's friendship with Donne may also have developed during his Hawstead period.[16] Although Donne himself would not enjoy the patronage of the Drurys until 1611, nor take orders until 1615, by the time of Hall's residency at Hawstead, Donne's religion was Anglican and his study theology. He may have found a congenial companion in the learned rector, who like himself had played the satirist in verse a half-dozen years earlier. In any case, by 1610, when the death of Drury's daughter Elizabeth moved Donne to compose the most elaborate funeral poems of the century, the two men were sufficiently acquainted that Hall could write prefatory verses to the *Anniversaries* and see the second of the two poems through the press while Donne was abroad in 1613.

While Hall's Hawstead years were productive they were also difficult. His stipend was small, his family growing; and, as he candidly confessed to his patron, he was forced to write books to buy them. And yet his writing and preaching did bring new opportunities. In 1605, desiring to inform himself of the condition of the Roman Church, he accompanied Sir Edmund Bacon abroad, visiting the cities of Brussels, Flushing, and Liège, concealing, not very successfully, his clerical garb beneath a green satin suit. In 1606 he made even greater friends. From a Mr. Gurrey, tutor to the Earl of Essex, Hall learned that his meditations had been well received at Richmond Palace, where Prince Henry, a zealous Protestant and like his royal father a keen student of theology, heard daily the sermons of notable English and foreign divines. Gurrey advised Hall to present himself at Richmond. Hall, ailing at the time and modest, first declined, then yielded to Gurrey's persuasions. His sermons were well received; and Hall was invited to become one of the twelve chaplains who preached to Prince Henry on a monthly basis.

In the meantime, relations between Hall and his patron Drury worsened. Although Hall's stipend was barely adequate to meet his needs, Sir Robert insisted on withholding the full amount of his salary.[17] Hall was inclined to remain at Hawstead, and he broached the matter of his stipend often, but Drury was stubborn. Finally, they had bitter words and Hall resolved to serve God elsewhere. The opportunity came in 1608 when he accepted the rectorship of Waltham in Norwich.

At Waltham, Hall found his situation much improved. He preached thrice weekly, continued to write, and as he grew in favor at court and in the eyes of his new patron, the Earl of Norwich, he won added preferment. In 1611 he became Archdeacon of Nottingham; in 1617, Dean of Worcester; and for a brief period he served as Prebendary of the Collegiate Church of Wolverhampton. Pluralism, or the practice of holding several church offices simultaneously, was much criticized in Hall's time because it left the pulpit of many a parish church empty or manned by incompetent curates who received niggardly wages from absentee rectors. But custom and ecclesiastical authority sanctioned the practice, and in accruing to himself additional honors, Hall was no different from many another clergyman of his time who found a way to make ends meet by holding multiple "livings."

During the same period Hall found another opportunity to travel abroad. In 1616 he accompanied Lord Viscount Doncaster on the latter's embassy to France, and in 1617 was one of the learned divines in the King's retinue to the Perth Conference in Scotland. This appointment was a singular honor, for James' intent was to persuade the Scots to accept an episcopal form of church government and thus bring the practice of the Scottish kirk into line with Anglican practice. Uniting the two kingdoms religiously as well as politically was an old dream of James', but it was a dream not easily realized. The dour Scots detested the very name of "bishop" and considered episcopal regalia and dignities a covert guise for political and religious oppression. Despite such fears, however, James had his way, and by authority of the General Assembly, bishops took their place, at least nominally, in the hierarchy of the Scottish kirk.

Although his moderate stance at the Conference won Hall friends among the Scottish clergy, he was criticized by his English colleagues for being overly tolerant of the Presbyterian position. Fearful of misrepresentation at home, Hall arranged to have himself immediately recalled to London, where he protested his loyalty to the King's satisfaction. To make his firm support of episcopacy even more conspicuous, Hall published the substance of his self-defence in *An Apology for the Church of England* (1619).

That James was confident of Hall's loyalty is evident in his appointment of Hall as a representative to the Synod of Dort the following year. This important conference, a confrontation between Calvinists and supporters of the Dutch theologian Arminius, aimed at resolving one of the most troublesome issues of the age, predestination, and defining once and for all the position of the reformed churches. Like James, Hall was Calvinist, seeing in the Arminian assertion that man acted freely in receiving or rejecting salvation a dangerous heresy. But Hall was also of a conciliatory nature, and his address to the convention won much applause for its moderation as well as for its polished Latin. Illness forced an early departure from the Synod, but Hall and other English theologians in attendance were granted handsome sums by the Dutch and each received gold medallions commemorating the event.

III *Hard Measure*

On the death of James in 1625, Hall lost a friend as well as a king; for with the accession of Charles I a new religious sensibility dominated the court and a new personality the church: William Laud. Hall's relations with Laud had always been cool. His Calvinism, his failure to emphasize ritual, and his moderation in controversy never set well with the shrewd and willful Laud, whose heart was set on a high-Anglican orthodoxy imposed by strenuous measures. But for some years a popular preacher, Hall had also through the years become one of the most eminent of English divines, and Laud advanced him despite their mutual antipathies. In 1624 Laud had offered Hall the bishopric of Gloucester, but he had declined. Three years later a new offer was extended and accepted. On 23 December 1627 Joseph Hall was consecrated Bishop of Exeter.

Hall's years at Exeter Cathedral were to be troubled ones. Suspected for his moderation by both Laud and the Puritans, he steered a perilous course between the two increasingly hostile factions, acquiescing to Laud's program of Romanizing Anglican ritual and liturgy, but tolerating the public preachers Laud considered subversive and taking no great interest in his superior's effort to expunge Puritan Sabbatarianism. Viewed objectively, Hall was a competent administrator, but complaints of his lack of rigor in the diocese were so intense on both sides that he contemplated at one point resigning his bishopric. He weathered the criticism, however, and at Laud's invitation put his pen to work again to refute the Scottish Presbyterians, who meanwhile had abrogated the Articles of Perth and had deposed the Scottish bishops.

Hall's compliance with Laud in this matter has been viewed by some historians as unprincipled and cowardly.[18] And it is true that Hall did submit both early draft and final version of his tract to the Archbishop, reshaping its argument to suit Laud and tempering remarks offensive to Catholics to please King Charles. But although Hall was by nature peace loving and obedient to those in authority, he was also deeply committed to episcopacy and the political hierarchy it presupposed. Like his old master, James I, Hall believed that the order of bishops was both ancient and divinely sanctioned and that its abrogation could only lead to confusion in both Church and State. Hall's *Episcopacy by Divine Right* (1640) was thus an eloquent affirmation of one of his most basic convictions.

In January 1640/1, Hall wrote a pamphlet entitled, "A Humble Remonstrance to the High Court of Parliament," furthering the thesis of *Episcopacy by Divine Right*. This pamphlet attracted the attention of five Presbyterian clergymen who in March of that year wrote a reply using the acronym "Smectymnuus." There followed an interchange between Hall and the Smectymnuans that climaxed with John Milton's entrance into the fray on behalf of the Presbyterian ministers. In Milton, Hall had a formidable opponent. Hall's junior by a number of years but already the author of several antiprelatical tracts, Milton was a master controversialist; and his "Animadversions upon the Remonstrant's Defence" contained a stinging personal attack on Hall. In the following years Hall and Milton traded more verbal blows in a series of vitriolic and abusive pamphlets that, while not uncharacteristic of religious polemics, make disturbing reading for modern partisans of the two authors. Although both men undoubtedly felt themselves vindicated in the controversy, the issue of ecclesiastical polity remained unresolved. By 1641 the question of Church government had become more than a religious issue.

Hall had, as a reward for his service in the debate with the dissenters, been created Bishop of Norwich. But during his tenure at Exeter, Parliament had become increasingly dominated by the Puritans; and they and the London crowds, weary of Laud's tyranny and suspicious of Charles' Catholic sympathies, were crying on all sides for Laud's arrest and the abolition of episcopal power. By December 1641 the hostility had grown to such an extent that bishops serving in the House of Lords refused to return to its chamber until their personal safety could be guaranteed. When Hall and other bishops appealed to the King, their letter was intercepted by Parliamentary agents and on 30 December 1641 Hall, Archbishop Williams of York, and eleven other bishops were arrested and sent to the Tower of London, charged with high treason.

Hall remained confined in the Tower until the middle of February when his release was authorized by the House of Lords. His freedom, however, was painfully brief. Upon learning that the bishops had been released, the House of Commons revoked bail, and Hall and the others were returned to the Tower, where he remained another six weeks until the Commons, realizing perhaps the insubstantiality of the indictment, granted the prisoners freedom.

Upon release, Hall went at once to Norwich to assume his duties as bishop. The diocese was strongly Puritan, and Bishop Wren, Hall's predecessor, had ruled with an iron hand that had aroused strong feeling on all sides. In a more peaceful time, a man of Hall's ability and moderation might have done much to settle the differences between opposing factions. Now it was too late for compromise. Hall enjoyed a brief period of peace, preaching regularly and administering the affairs of the diocese; but by August 1641 Charles was in the field, the Civil War had begun, and by late March of 1643, Parliament passed the ordinance of sequestration, depriving Hall of his bishopric and his living.

Of the privation and indignities of these years, Hall gives vivid account in his autobiographical *Hard Measure*. There he describes the seizure of his rents and household goods, the constant threat of arrest, and the profanation of the cathedral church by an unruly company of Roundheads bent on effacing the relics of Popery:

Lord, what work was here! what clattering of glasses! what beating down of walls! what tearing up of monuments! what pulling down of seats! what wresting out of irons and brass from the windows and graves! what defacing

of arms! what demolishing of curious stonework, that had not any represen-
tation in the world but only of the cost of the founder and the skill of the
mason! what tooting and piping upon the organ-pipes and what a hideous
triumph on the market-day before all the country, when, in a kind of
sacrilegious and profane procession, all the organ-pipes, vestments, both
copes and surplices, together with the leaden cross which had been newly
sawn down from over the Greenyard pulpit, and the service books and
singing-books that could be had, were carried to the fire in the public mar-
ket-place; a lewd wretch walking before the train in his cope trailing in the
dirt, with a service-book in his hand, imitating in an impious scorn the tune,
and usurping the words of the litany used formerly in the church.[19]

During Cromwell's rule, Hall was allowed to preach, but not to
ordain, and although he was promised an allowance by the Puritan
authorities, it was never forthcoming and he was forced to subsist on
the income of his wife and the sale of his books. When he was finally
ejected from the episcopal residence in 1648, he and his family
moved to a small house at Higham, a few miles distant. There he
lived privately and securely for the remaining years of his life,
preaching occasionally but writing constantly. He died 8 September
1656, and was buried the following day in the parish church, without pomp as his will directed.[20]

IV Hall and Humanism

In his *Worthies of England* Thomas Fuller wrote of Hall, "He may
be said to have died with his pen in his hand, whose writing and
living expired together."[21] The sentiment, which would not have
been a bad epitaph, reminds us that Hall, among other things, was a
man of letters and a pioneer in several literary genres. To appreciate
his authorship, his work must be viewed as a whole. What is needed
is an approach to Hall that acknowledges the diversity of his efforts
while recognizing the essential unity of his purpose as an author.

One way to achieve such a view is to place Hall in the tradition in
which as an author he belongs, that of Renaissance Humanism. This
tradition, with its concern for Greek and Roman antiquities, its
doctrine of literary imitation, and its practice of using classical literary forms as vehicles for Christian themes, was the major intellectual movement of the sixteenth century.[22] It encompassed, of
course, more than Hall embraced. Preferring to spend his writer's
apprenticeship with the cankered and severely moralistic muse of
satire than with the Ovidian narrative or Virgilian pastoral, he for-

went thereafter secular verse and devoted his considerable literary talents to moral instruction and religious polemics. But while Hall's Puritan leanings made him scorn the secular spirit of Humanism, he accepted one of its major premises: the congeniality of classical learning and Christian culture. Hall's Humanism can be seen in his devotion to literary imitation, his reverence for classical moralists, and his concern for style, while his satirical temper, piety, and commitment to scholarship and the active life recall Erasmus, one of the greatest of Renaissance Humanists and a favorite of Hall's.

Humanism suggests as well an approach to Hall's work. He was not what we would now call an original thinker. He was, rather, a stylist, who began with a model. To understand Hall's achievements we must know his models and understand his methods, for Hall held imitation superior to invention, seeing in the former not servile copying or plagiarism but a judicious and artful adaptation of traditional form for a new and sometimes better use.[23] His view was in no way unique. Imitation was central to classical theories of rhetoric and poetics and what the ancients prescribed the Humanists tended to endorse.[24] In both theory and practice, Hall became the author his Cambridge education had prepared him to become.

It is also necessary to understand Hall's conception of style. Humanism fostered a rhetorical culture, preoccupied with expression and convinced that words were as important as matter. Bacon was to deny the premise and develop a prose style repudiating the swelling Ciceronian periods the earlier Humanists admired and imitated. But the importance Bacon attached to style suggests he shared the Humanist assumption that style was not just ornament but a philosophical statement. Hall's "Senecan Amble" should therefore be approached not merely as a way of writing but as a way of thinking. As a leader in the anti-Ciceronian movement, Hall, like Bacon, played an important part in fitting English expression to the intellectual demands of the modern world.

Finally, it is necessary to understand Hall's Christianity, for he reveals the characteristic Humanist bias for ethics rather than metaphysics. The English Humanists were, for the most part, schoolmasters, either by profession or inclination. Hostile to the abstruse speculation of medieval theologians, they viewed education as a species of moral instruction and the Greek and Roman classics as a library of essential information on ethics, politics, psychology, and philosophy. Hall, like other Humanists, often quarreled with the ancients, especially when his revealed religion came into conflict with the reason of philosophers or morality of poets. But his conviction was that much of pagan thought could be accommodated to Christian practice. In the Humanist tradition, then, Hall was very much the schoolmaster, and his authorship an extension of pastoral care. He wrote nothing that was not edifying, useful for the correction of vice or the raising of men's minds to God or the freeing of men's minds from error. To moderns such concerns are intellectual curiosities, but Hall's principles, theological and literary, were the verities of his age. They provided the motive for his writing, gave meaning to his life and coherence to his efforts as an author. If Hall—as literary innovator, stylist, and defender of his faith—were less interesting than he was our time would still be well spent in studying a man who makes so accessible the major premises of his age.

CHAPTER 2

The First English Satirist

S ATIRE is a sullen art, exuding so little sweetness or light that
Hall's contemporaries likened it to surgery or thought it
medicinal.[1] It was the duty of the satirist to strip away the appearance of moral health, expose the festering sore of vice and folly, and
apply the caustic that would cleanse the body politic of infection.
Righteous indignation was the characteristic tone of satire, ridicule
its basic strategy. Accordingly, although the satirist himself was
rarely a popular figure, his satires were often a sensation.

In late Elizabethan England satire was a fashionable, if minor,
genre. It assumed many forms, and its roots, as Hallett Smith reminds us, were social and economic: satire both mirrored and grew
out of the conditions of its age.[2] But it was also the product of
literary tradition, and for Hall, thoroughly schooled in Humanist
principles, the writing of satire was both an academic exercise and a
literary apprenticeship requiring imitation, observation, and mas-
tery of language. He conceived of his art narrowly, choosing as
models the great satirists of antiquity, Juvenal, Persius, Horace, and
Lucian. Satire was thus as much an expression of his interest in
classical learning as of his revulsion at the decadence of his times.

I Virgidemiae

On 31 March 1597 a slender volume of verse was registered with
the Stationer's Company of London under the title *Virgidemiarum,
First Three Books of Toothless Satires.*[3] Hall was then in his
twenty-third year, a fellow of Emmanuel College; and as was often
the custom among authors who did not consider themselves professional writers, the poems were published anonymously. A second
volume, containing three books of *Biting Satires,* was published the
following year. With this "harvest of switches," or so Hall's Latin

25

title might be translated,[4] Hall established himself as an
Elizabethan satirist.

That Hall conceived of the publication of the *Virgidemiae* as an
auspicious literary event is clear from the first lines of its verse
prologue:

> I first adventure, with fool-hardy might
> To tread the steps of perilous despight:
> I first adventure: follow me who list,
> And be the second English Satirist. (I, i, 1–4)

Hall's claim to priority as a satirist has often been challenged, for if
satire be broadly defined, then he was preceded in his own century
by Skelton, Gascoigne, and Lodge, among others, each of whom
criticized vice and folly in verse. But if, on the other hand, satire is
more narrowly conceived as a species of poetry governed by the
example of classical authors, then Hall's claim is more firmly
grounded, for no English satirist before Hall had so successfully
imitated the form or captured the spirit of Roman models.

In writing such satire, Hall was in the intellectual mainstream of
his time, for the imitation of classical authors was the chief endeavor
of Renaissance Humanism. As a university man and skilled Latinist,
he had read and doubtlessly admired the satirists of the Romans'
Silver Age; and as a young man with strong moral sense and a keen
eye for social detail, he must have marked in the Roman satirists'
efforts a challenge to check the affectation and corruption of
Elizabethan London in a similar fashion. The *Virgidemiae,* then,
despite their presentation to the reading public as unique, were in
fact one of many expressions of the late sixteenth-century interest in
classical literary forms.

Recognizing that Hall's satires were an exercise in literary imitation accounts for the special character of the *Virgidemiae.* In form,
Hall's iambic pentameter couplets come as close as English prosody
might to the Latin distich, the common meter of Roman satire.
Moreover, Hall's intention to sear the vices and follies of his time in
a carefully controlled poetic medium was identical to that of the
Roman satirist to whose example Hall was most indebted, Juvenal.
Juvenal's caustic verses offered a grim excursion through the seamy
side of Roman life, a plethora of graphic details, a *locus classicus* for

what Alvin Kernan has described as the characteristic mis-en-scène of satire:

The scene of satire is always disorderly and crowded, packed to the very point of bursting. The deformed faces of depravity, stupidity, greed, venality, ignorance, and maliciousness group closely together for a moment, stare boldly out at us, break up, and another tight knot of figures collects, stroking full stomachs, looking vacantly into space, nervously smiling at the great, proudly displaying jewels and figures, clinking moneybags, slyly fingering new-bought fashions. The scene is equally choked with things: ostentatious buildings and statuary, chariots, sedan-chairs, clothes, books, food, horses, dildoes, luxurious furnishings, gin bottles, wigs. Pick up any major satiric work and open it at random and the immediate effect is one of disorderly profusion.[5]

Hall's *Virgidemiae* depict a not dissimilar scene; and both manner and method were conventional. Like other Elizabethans, Hall took wit, obscurity, melancholy, and scurrility to be as fundamental to satire as lofty thoughts and elevated diction to epic; and like some other satirists of the period, he identified satire with "satyr," supposing the words etymologically akin and therefore suggestive of satire's proper ethos and decorum. As he observed in his "Post-Script to the Reader": "It is not for every one to relish a true and natural satire, being of itself besides the native and inbred bitterness and tartness of particulars, both hard of concept and harsh of style." But if the *Virgidemiae* are classical in form and method, they are also thoroughly Elizabethan in atmosphere; for from their crabbed syntax leer a gallery of social types, a dozen characteristic abuses, Hall and his contemporaries knew from experience. Hall's occasional borrowings and general indebtedness to Juvenal and Persius notwithstanding, the *Virgidemiae* were a singular debut for a young author.

Hall describes the first three books of *Virgidemiae* as "toothless" satires, a term Milton was to view contemptuously as a contradiction in terms.[6] But the toothlessness of Hall's verses pertains more to their matter than to the degree of Hall's indignation; for while the abuses he treats are lamentable, they are hardly vicious, dealing as they do with the state of literature, the decay of poetry, and the corruption of the professions rather than reaching down to the murkier depths of other public and private vices.

Book I surveys the late Elizabethan literary scene: the first of its nine satires, a "program" satire modelled loosely on Juvenal I,[7] both blasts a half-dozen literary vices and announces Hall's purpose as a satirist. He does not write, he boldly declares, silly romances about wandering knights and wanton ladies, flattering sonnets, or easy pastorals. He does not compose purple passages or melodramatic "scenes" to appeal only to grosser tastes. He cannot bring himself to "writhe" his "fawning tail/To some great Patron" (I, i, 11–2). His intention, rather, is correction: to "check the mis-ordered world, and lawless times" (I, i, 24). This disorder Hall conceives mythically in the second satire of Book I as the deflowering of the Muses, an outrage that has led to the total corruption of these traditional personifications of poetic inspiration:

> Now is Parnassus turned to the stews,
> And on Bay-stocks the wanton Myrtle grows.
> Cytheron hill's become a Brothel-bed,
> And Pyrene sweet, turned to a poisoned head
> Of coal-black puddle: whose infectious stain
> Corrupteth all the lowly fruitful plain. (I, ii, 17–22)

For Hall, chief locus of this infection was the theater. Satire iii provides a graphic sketch of a stalking Tamburlaine whose "thundering threats" and "big-sounded sentences" are punctuated by the ludicrous antics of a clown, while satire iv lays the blame for such aesthetic outrages at the feet of moneygrubbing playwrights who pander to the taste of groundlings with sloppy verse and "worme-ate stories of old time." Hall's censure is strong—a modern reader is likely to find it excessively so—but Hall's criticism is hardly unique. Sir Philip Sidney in his *Apology for Poetry* (written c.1581) had also faulted the contemporary stage for its conflation of tragedy and comedy, which to his classical sensibilities violated both decorum and reason; and like other Elizabethans Hall was contemptuous of the fantastic tales of magicians, enchantments, and forlorn maidens, filched casually from Ariosto and other Italian romances of chivalry then in vogue throughout Europe. Yet although Hall condemns the unrestrained imagination, he allows the "ancient right" of poets and painters to invent; and he is careful to exempt from his censure Edmund Spenser, "whom no earthly wight/Dares once to emulate, much less dares despight" (I, iv, 23–4).

The remaining satires of Book I focus on the defects of contemporary verse. Satire v casts a scornful eye on lugubrious "complaint" literature made popular by the success of Sackville and Norton's *The Mirror for Magistrates*, a collection of narrative poems first published in 1559 which treats the misfortunes of famous persons and carries doleful warnings to their readers; and satire vi ridicules poets who try to write English verse according to the rules of Latin prosody, foolishly supposing that if they achieve "the numbered verse that Virgil sung," then "Virgil self shall speak the English tongue." The final three satires aim respectively at flattering sonneteers, profane treatments of religious themes, and writers who practice "experimental bawdery" in erotic narratives. Of particular interest is Hall's commentary on love poetry in satire vii, the final lines of which exude a Donne-like cynicism:

> Then can he term his dirty ill-faced bride
> Lady and Queen, and virgin deified:
> Be she all sooty-black, or berry-brown,
> She's white as morrow's milk, or flakes new blown.
> And though she be some dunghill drudge at home,
> Yet can he her resign some refuse room
> Amidst the well-known stars: or if not there,
> Sure will he Saint her in his Calendar. (I, vii, 19–26)

Because of its practical criticism, the first book of Hall's satires has remained the most often read, and much scholarly energy has been expended in identifying the poets and playwrights criticized. Besides Marlow, clearly indicated by the allusion to his famous protagonist, Tamburlaine, Hall probably had Drayton and Daniel in mind in his attack on "doleful legends," although the details of satire v are inconclusive, and almost certainly had Robert Southwell and his *St. Peter's Complaint* (1595) in mind in the censure of religious poetry. Hall's obscene writers were probably Robert Greene and Thomas Nashe. Yet the convention that permitted Hall to attack fellow authors in satire also required that such attacks be obscure, and Hall's diagnosis of faulty poetic "kinds" may be more important than the identification of offending authors. In any event, the satire is quite respectable as practical criticism, evidence of Hall's wide reading, and grounded in traditional premises—an insistence on classical decorum and propriety in poetry and honesty in poets.

The seven satires of Book II show Hall's awareness of the social and economic conditions of his time. Specifically, they deal with the professions of Elizabethan society: authors, scholars, lawyers, physicians, clergymen, chaplain-tutors, and astrologers. Hall's theme is that these groups—and by implication society as a whole—are wrongheaded. Authors write much but know nothing, scholars go unrewarded, greedy lawyers thrive on crime, and physicians charge much but cure few. Unemployed clergy must scrounge for benefices or chaplaincies and endure the scorn and low wages of stingy squires. Finally the astrologer ("our artist") foretells the weather but does nothing about those misfortunes his foreknowledge, were it genuine, might prevent:

> In the heaven's universal Alphabet,
> All earthly things so surely are foreset,
> That who can read those figures, may foreshow
> What ever thing shall afterwards ensue.
> Fain would I know (might it our Artist please)
> Why can his tell-troth *Ephemerides*
> Teach him the weather's state so long beforn:
> And not foretell him, nor his fatal horn,
> Nor his death's-day, nor so such sad event,
> Which he might wisely labor to prevent? (II, vii, 1–10)

Book III is a critique of manners. Like many of his contemporaries, Hall believed that civilization was on the decline and had been so since Adam's transgression had caused both mankind and nature to fall. Hall expresses this view in the first satire of this series by contrasting the present time with the mythical Golden Age, a primitive epoch of abundance, simplicity, and innocence. For the details of the myth Hall was indebted to a number of classical sources, chiefly to the *Hippolytus* of Seneca and the pseudo-Senecan *Octavia*. But the idea of using the myth as a foil to contemporary ills was probably suggested by Juvenal, who in his sixth satire envisioned the decline of values as the retreat of Justice and her sister Charity to the Heavens. In Hall's rendition of the myth, however, the primal innocence of the "world's best days" is seen first sophisticated by the invention of agriculture and metallurgy and finally depraved by human greed, pride, and covetousness. Man's total corruption is signaled by his belief that he is a "god at least" and demonstrated in his boldness in ravaging nature's store. Hall asks,

O Nature, was the world ordained for nought,
But fill man's maw, and feed man's idle thought.
(III, i, 56–7)

This satire, some of the best poetry Hall wrote, prefaces a series
of vignettes and character sketches of Elizabethan personality types.
As classical tradition permits, Hall ascribes to each a fictitious name.
Great Osmond (sat. ii) erects a huge and protentious tomb that his
name may not be forgotten, a "courteous Citizen" (sat. iii) pleads
with Hall to accept an invitation to dinner and then resents it when
the invitation is accepted, Polemon and Myson (sat. iv) are big
spenders whose conspicuous consumption conceals their real lack of
charity and benevolence. A lusty courtier (sat. v) makes himself
ridiculous by wearing a fashionable but absurd wig and bonnet; the
alcoholic Gullion (sat. vi) drinks the Acheron dry while Charon must
wait until Guillon's "bladder would unload" (1. 20) before the hellish
boatman can continue his journey. The dandy Ruffio (sat. vii), "all
trapped in the new-found bravery of several nations," works to conceal the rumblings of an empty stomach.

The first satire of the second series (Books IV–VI) is a defense of
Hall's methods. Sardonically, he anticipates the response of readers
who, puzzling over his crabbed lines and "scoring the margent with
his blazing stars/And hundred crooked interlinears," will in dismay
toss them into the dust heap. The more discerning, however, recognizing that "the best lies low, and loathes the shallow view"
(1. 20), will read again. Hall protests the idea that his obscurity
should be flailed while the vicious persons he exposes remain
anonymous and speculates that if he were to speak more plainly,
"signal out and say once flat and plain," he would get a quick reaction. With a wealth of comic detail, he describes the grimace of
Titus the fortune hunter when his schemes have been laid bare by
Hall's cankered muse:

Now see I fire-flakes sparkle from his eyes
Like a comet's tail in the angry skies,
His pouting cheeks puff up above his brow
Like a swollen Toad touched with the Spider's blow:
His mouth shrinks sideward like a scornful Playse
To take his tired Ear's ungrateful place;
His Ears hang lauing like a new-lugged swine
To take some counsel of his grieved eyen. (IV, i, 66–73)

But Hall welcomes such a response:

> Now laugh I loud, and break my spleen to see
> This pleasing pastime of my poesie. (IV, i, 74–75)

Declaring that his earlier satires were but "toothless toys" and as "lightning to a thunder-clap," Hall drops the reader into a demi-monde of brothels, strumpets, lecherous husbands and faithless wives, sexual excess and perversion. Cyneds "neighs after Bridals and fresh maidenhead"; Caia furnishes her impotent husband with an heir while the bribed midwife marvels at the resemblance "the bastard babe doth bear his father's face." Lena plays the close adulteress by night, the chaste dame by day, while her syphilitic lover writhes in agony.

While satiric convention does not bind Hall to thematic continuity, Hall's exposé of sexual misconduct is a clue to his intention in the remainder of Books IV–VI. Such misconduct is generally another instance of the decay in values which according to Hall plagues his age. More particularly it is an example of the profound disorder that exists in the most basic of human institutions, the family. If sacred matrimony cannot induce faith and trust, where can these virtues be found? Certainly not in the relation of father to son, for as satire ii of Book IV makes clear, natural affection has been undermined by ambition and greed. Other satires in Book IV touch on the same gloomy note of social and personal degeneracy. In his finely drawn portrait of Gallio (sat. iv) Hall prophesies that this gluttonous, effeminate dandy, if he marries, will produce only pygmies like himself; and his condemnation of usury (sat. v) is at the same time a long lament over the decline of generosity in his age. Now thousands live by others' loss, shady deals, extortion, and deceptive bankruptcies: "Whatever sickly sheep so secret dies/But some foul Raven hath bespoke his eyes?"

Another symptom of the decadence of the times is the loss of man's place in the social order. Now, Hall complains, men do not accept their lot, and to their sorrow. Plowmen turn soldier in hopes of easy money and adventure only to find war not as sweet as the expectation, small town burghers get rich dishonestly and then fear robbery, homebodies excited by traveler's tales sail to faraway places and learn first hand of the tedium and perils of real travel. Finally, Hall turns his attention to religion, contrasting the glory of

classical Rome to the foolish pomp and circumstance of the Holy
City of the Roman Church and imagining how Juvenal ("Aquines")
might wonder at such scenes of Papist practice:

> When once I think if carping Aquines spright
> To see now Rome, were licensed to the light;
> How his enraged Ghost would stamp and stare
> That Caesar's throne is turned to Peter's Chair.
> To see an old shorn lozell perched high
> Crossing beneath a golden Canopy,
> The whiles a thousand hairless crownes crouch low
> To kiss the precious case of his proud toe. (IV, vii, 9–16)

The four satires of Book V present a specifically Elizabethan picture and are therefore of greater interest to one curious about the
conditions of Hall's times. Like the satires of Book IV, they form
another grim chapter in the history of social decline, but their fundamental focus is on social abuses: the cruelty of landlords (i), the
decay in hospitality among the gentry (ii), the evils of enclosure (iii),
and the expense of living in cities (iv). In no other book of the
Virgidemiae does Hall examine the texture of Elizabethan society
with such scrutiny. Surely no other book demonstrates how much of
his own experience is brought to bear in his satires.

Although only a young man when he wrote the *Virgidemiae*, Hall
was a keen observer, and his knowledge of rural economics had
been formed firsthand. As the son of the local bailiff, he knew of the
system of rents, fees, fines, and tributes that constituted the nexus
of tenant-landlord relations; he had seen the sobering effects of
rent-racking on the Leicestershire poor, and if his depiction of their
plight is caustic, there is also more than a little sympathy for the
victims of the landlords' cruelty. Time was, Hall insists, when rents
were nominal, or at least reasonable; now property owners, whose
wealth may have been acquired only recently or through some
fraudulent claims or forged document, raise a tenant's rent "to double trebles of his one year's price" (i, 58) and reduce him to the most
abject poverty. Hall illuminates this sad condition with sharply-
limned miniatures, capturing the circumstances of the isolated cottage dweller:

> Whose thatched spars are furred with sluttish soot
> A whole inch thick, shining like Black-moor's brows

Through smoke that down the headless barrel blows.
At his beds-feet feed his stalled team
His swine beneath, his pullen o'er the beam
A starved Tenement, such as I guess,
Stand straggling in the wastes of Holderness,
Or such as shiver on a Peake-hill side,
When March's lungs beat on their turf-clad hide. (V, i, 60–68)

Harsh monosyllables and a halting rhythm underscore Hall's bitterness; this is no matter for sweet lyrics. Yet despite such wretched living conditions, the tenant must still as custom dictates regale his landlord at each harvest festival with capons, cheeses, fruits, and other products of his industry; for, as Hall cynically notes, "whom cannot gifts at last cause to relent/Or to win favor, or flee punishment?" In recompense, the typical patron makes empty promises; and even the tenant of many years, "Tho much he spent in the rotten roof's repair/In hope to have it left unto his heir," may be abruptly ousted and packed off to the colonies if the landlord sees it to his advantage to turn arable land to pasture for his sheep. In anticipation of Oliver Goldsmith's famous theme (in "The Deserted Village"), the satire fittingly concludes with the image of a decaying village and ruined church, whose steeple is the last and ironic vestige of the sacrilege of lands foreclosed and enclosed:

Would it not vex thee where thy sires did keep
To see the dunged folds of dag-tailed sheep,
And ruined house where holy things were said,
Whose freestone walls the thatched roof upbraid,
Whose shrill Saints-bell hangs on his louerie,
While the rest are damned to the Plumbery?
Yet pure devotion lets the steeple stand,
And idle battlements on either hand;
Least that perhaps, were all those relics gone,
Furious his sacrilege could not be known. (V, i, 115–24)

To Hall, the decline in hospitality, like the abuses of landlords, was a symptom of social decay. It represented a departure from time-honored custom and was caused in part by the flight of the gentry to London, which in turn resulted in poorly maintained estates and economically depressed countrysides. "Housekeeping is dead, Saturio," Hall intones to his fictional companion in satire ii,

proceeding then on an excursion through "Breakneckshire" where
the pair seeks a free meal in an imposing mansion with gilded ex-
terior. The great house offers little hospitality, however. No dogs
bark, no porter opens the gate, all is "dumb and silent, like the dead
of night." The marble pavement is overrun with weeds, "keep out"
is written in broad Greek letters above the door, and poverty, once
the uninvited but inevitable guest of the lowly cottage, now begins
"to revel it in Lordly hallo." Speaking directly, Hall advises gallants
to spend their money on hospitality and maintenance of their estates
rather than on expensive and useless finery. The satire concludes
with a vignette, probably inspired by Juvenal and Jonsonian in
comic detail and ironic tone: Poor Trebius enjoys the hospitality of
"lavish" Virro, but the hospitality is ungraciously extended. Trebius
is seated at the lower end of the table, provided with leftovers and a
pauper's diet while Virro gorges himself on dainties and guzzles the
finest wines. Then, Trebius is scorned by a jealous waiter, ridiculed
for his rude table etiquette, and finally ushered without ceremony
from the room before he has had a chance to finish his meal. Yet
Hall, with delightful irony, inquires if it is not enough for Trebius to
be able to say he dined at a rich man's table?

After some general comments on satires and the "brittle ears" of
his contemporaries who cannot bear to hear themselves criticized,
Hall focuses on the evils of enclosure, a common literary topic and a
persistent political issue from the time of Skelton and More on-
wards. Hall approaches the theme in a characteristic fashion, by
contrasting past with present. He observes that earlier generations
of Englishmen erected no fences, but marked the boundaries of
their freeholds with simple stones and crosses. Now men, more
complicated and less trusting, build walls of mud, sticks, stones, and
bricks. "Do so," Hall exclaims,

> So be, thou stake not up the common stile,
> So be thou hedge in nought, but what's thine own,
> So be thou pay what tithes thy neighbor's done
> So be thou let not lie in fallowed plane
> That which was wont yield usury of grain. (V, iii, 65–9)

Recalling the "happier days of old Deucalion," when the mythical
counterpart of Noah inhabited the world alone, its only landlord,
Hall's anger rises at the plight of the industrious peasant who cannot

pay an enormous sum to harvest the remainder of his crop, his new-mown field halved by some rich man's fence.

The fourth satire of Book V is a brief vignette. Like others in this series, it aims at economic abuses. Villius, a wealthy farmer, leaves his son twenty pounds per year, which his simple neighbors praise as a handsome inheritance. But, like many of his generation, the son goes off to the city, spends his fortune on wife, wardrobe, servants, and other luxuries so that his capital is quickly exhausted. Hall concludes that "forty pounds serve not the farmer's heir."

The sixth and final book of *Virgidemiae* consists of a single poem, a mock recantation of the rest. C. S. Lewis praised it as an "admirable ironic idea" and an example of the "power of an organizing idea to make what might have been a mere heap of poetry into a poem."[8] This evaluation is sound. Hall's method is to underscore the theme of modern degeneracy by supposing the present age superior to the past both in morals and poetry. "Was never age I ween so pure as this," he proclaims as, with thinly veiled irony, he absolves his age of those vices he has earlier taken great pains to denounce. Thieves, drunkards, liars simply cannot be found; merchants are now honest, patrons generous, parasites nonexistent. Moreover, the men of Hall's age are not only paragons of virtue (rather than the laggards and scoundrels he has previously charged), but modern authors are superior to the ancients in wit. Just see, Hall exclaims enthusiastically, with what skill contemporary poets can write eulogies on the death of dogs, cats, and birds, or praise folly and baldness ("What do not fine wits dare to undertake?"). By such indirect methods Hall ridicules the witlessness of Elizabethan poetasters who turn out turgid Roman legends or chivalric romance, tawdry imitations of Virgil and Petrarch, or filch whole passages from modern authors like Erasmus, while Hall's arch-critic Labeo is singled out for his incompetence and special talents as a plagiarist.

Its obscure style and veiled allusion notwithstanding, the *Virgidemiae* is a singular accomplishment. Not all the pieces of this satiric anthology are, of course, of even quality; Hall's ranting is occasionally boring or forced, his portraiture sometimes a kind of cliché. Yet there are flashes of brilliance. We think for instance of Hall's finely wrought description of the golden age (III, i), or his account of "Old Lollio" (IV, ii), who plays the miser and usurer to make his wastrel son into a gentleman. The son shows no gratitude for such sacrifice, only shame when some companion mentions his father's name; finally, when the son is established as a rent-racking squire, Old Lollio's name is obliterated by a false pedigree that insures his posterity's social security. It is a poignant little sketch, diffuse but entertaining and insightful. The lines describing Lollio's impoverished dress are in the finest tradition of Roman satire; while Hall's treatment of the old man's ambition for his son and his son's anxiety and rejection of his father is cynical but knowing.

The *Virgidemiae* were reprinted in 1602, and Milton recalled them briefly to public attention in his quarrel with Hall in 1640. Thereafter, until Pope's admiration inspired eighteenth-century interest and new editions,[9] the satires were largely forgotten. Yet if, as the proverb goes, imitation is the sincerest form of flattery, Hall's effort to write Juvenalian satire in English was much approved by his contemporaries. Between the publication of the first three books of *Virgidemiae* in 1597 and the official condemnation of all satires in June 1599, a number of collections similar to Hall's appeared. Chief of these were John Marston's *The Metamorphosis of Pigmalion's Image* (1598) and *The Scourge of Villanie* (1598),[10] William Rankins' *Seven Satyrs* (1598), and Thomas Middleton's *Microcynicon* (1599). Hall's satires are superior to these in detail, in versification, and in capturing the spirit of his Roman models. Like all satires, the *Virgidemiae* reflect, although darkly, their times; yet Hall's vision is surprisingly full and articulate. Only the comic drama of the period provides a more colorful or entertaining impression of vagaries of Elizabethan culture; and while Hall may be faulted for his calculated obscurity, the weave of his satire is no more complicated than the age whose folly he decried. Except perhaps for the satires of Donne, Hall's are the most accomplished of their kind written in England before Dryden gave a high finish to the genre and Pope perfected it.

II   Mundus Alter et Idem

Sometime late in his residence at Cambridge, or in the years immediately following, Hall tried his hand at a prose satire in Latin, *Mundus Alter et Idem* ("A World, Different yet the Same"). Perhaps to avoid the government's edict against satires, *Mundus* carried the imprint of Frankfort (c. 1605), although it may have been printed in London. Sometime later John Healey, like Hall an alumnus of Emmanuel College, translated *Mundus* into English.[11] Healey's translation, *The Discovery of a New World,* was entered on the Stationer's Register 18 January 1609.

Hall's authorship of the *Mundus* has sometimes been questioned. The work appeared anonymously, and German translations of 1613 and 1704 name Alberico Gentili as author. Healey, however, identifies the author by his initials ("I. H.") and describes him as a "reverend man." Most importantly, while Hall himself never admitted authorship, neither did he deny it when Milton made Hall's composing of satires a scandal in the Smectymnuan controversy of 1640–2. That the work is Hall's is now generally accepted.[12]

Hall's satire relates the experiences of the itinerant scholar Mercurius Britannicus in Antarctica, a continent about which little was known in Hall's day. Through his narrator, Hall describes the appearance and customs of the Antarcticans and contrasts and compares these with European manners and morals. Numerous references to authorities real and invented give the narration a semblance of veracity, but Hall's purpose is clear: to burlesque traveler's tales then in vogue; to ridicule gluttons, drunkards, domineering women, Papists, fools; and to entertain through grotesque caricature and scatalogical details. The work must not be taken too seriously; undoubtedly it provided Hall with a much needed vacation from academic routine.

Hall's satire begins with a dialogue between Mercurius and two of his friends: Peter Beroaldus, a Frenchman, and Adrian Cornelius Droge, a Dutchman. Their conversation touches upon the rewards of travel, differences in the various European languages, and the proposal of Mercurius that they prove the existence of a large and undiscovered continent mysteriously alluded to in the writings of Seneca. After some attempt to dissuade him from the adventure, Mercurius' friends agree to accompany him on the voyage and all three set sail on a ship, appropriately named the *Fantasia*. When Beroaldus and Droge are detained in their respective homelands, Mercurius, to avoid the derision of friends, decides to brave the dangers of the journey alone, and after two years arrives in Antarctica.

From there, Hall's satire follows a simple outline. Mercurius' itinerary takes him to four imaginary kingdoms, each exhibiting some preposterous moral disorder: *Crapulia*, the land of gluttons; *Viraginia*, a land of shrews; *Moronia*, a land of fools; and *Lavernia*, land of thieves. Each of these territories has provinces indicating the subspecies of the four major disorders and principal cities, villages, and a terrain suggesting the character of each folly. The allegory is

not systematic: Hall's is a kind of hit-and-run caricature grounded
not so much on philosophical principle as in a practical observation
of men and manners. There is, however, a dominant theme. The
ancients had supposed the Antipodes, by definition upside down, a
land in which the order of nature was likewise reversed. Hall's
Antipodeans do not stand on their heads, but their values are
ludicrously inverted.

In Crapulia, Mercurius observes strange beasts, curious rivers,
oddly constructed cities, and bizarre islands; but the moral atmosphere evoked is that of an Elizabethan tavern: a riot of gluttony and
dyspepsia. The inhabitants of one of its provinces, Phamphagonia,
devote themselves wholly to eating, choose governors for their girth
(rather than for their beards as in Europe, Mercurius notes dryly),
and honor Apicius, the most notorious gormand of antiquity, as the
patron of their academies. In another province, Yrionia, reveling
and quaffing are the first order of business, sobriety is forbidden,
and the worship of Bacchus mandatory. The populations, laws, and
customs of both provinces are presented to the reader in a wealth of
Rabelaisian detail—groaning tables and full mugs, spitoons and
chamber pots, swollen flesh and choleric humors. But Hall's moral
bias is clear in the scatological implications of the names of his
mythical provinces and in the gross ugliness of their inhabitants.
Mercurius tells us that "the young women may not marry until such
time as before a bench of matrons, they make a public demonstra-
tion to their husbands that shall be, that their dugs and chins may
meet without forcing of either." (Healey's translation)

While wandering on the frontiers of Crapulia, Mercurius is seized
by a rout of women and taken into Viraginia, where he is interro-
gated, imprisoned, and finally paroled after swearing never to interrupt, contradict, or slander the fair sex. Here, Hall's purpose is to
satirize proverbial vices of women such as garrulousness, inconstancy, vanity, and a desire to dominate men by imagining a land
where sexual roles are reversed, where women rule and men per-
form domestic chores and answer to their wives' every whim. Hall's
view of this monstrous government of women is what one might
expect from an author of his sex and era: Mercurius is aghast at the
spectacle of men sweeping, washing, weaving, and carding, timo-
rously tiptoeing to their wives' beds on demand, and humbly sub-
mitting to ridicule, regular beatings and the filthiest of living conditions—the folly of all of which he sees reflected in the barren fields

and unmaintained cities of the land. Hall's satire, however, has a double edge. We are informed that all Viraginians are immigrants; while some Viraginian women have fled hither to wear the pants, most have come as refugees from their husbands' abuse. Moreover, a sympathy for the condition of honest women is implied in the tender feelings some Viraginians feel for their downtrodden mates and in the picture of men as a propertyless class, victims of sexual abuse and public scorn, which is after all simply an image of European society in reverse. That Viraginia is Europe through a glass darkly is suggested at the conclusion of the second book where Mercurius' escape from the land of women is facilitated by the directions of the many of his countrymen he has encountered there.

Moronia, the land of fools, is the largest and most populated of Hall's fictional kingdoms. Like other Antipodeans, the Moronians are driven by aberrations in their manner of government, the design of their cities, and in their own appearance. In one subdivision, where fickleness is the dominant humor (significantly, it is adjacent to Viraginia), forms of government are altered at a whim, cities are constructed on casters, and opinions, friends, and even wives are changed daily. In another province, where melancholy reigns, a dark and slovenly people given to private fantasies and mutual hostilities haunt a forbidding terrain of frost and crag. And in yet another, dominated by credulity, an ignorant and downtrodden peasantry occupies an uncultivated land of monasteries, idols, superstitious practice and priestly arrogance.

The final stop on Mercurius' itinerary is Lavernia, a land of thieves. The inhabitants of this infertile but affluent land make do by legerdemain, trickery, and extortion; and their society is characterized appropriately by fortified households, locked coffers, and fear and insecurity. Here children are taught filching from birth and keep in practice by stealing dirt or fence posts from neighboring fields. Hall's depiction of Lavernia has the same preposterous elements and droll comedy as that of other Antarctic lands; but, as elsewhere in *Mundus*, the distortions of Lavernia are only oblique reflections of European vice. Mercurius finds the land filled with lawyers, alchemists, and monuments to plagiarized and plagiarizing poets; and, as elsewhere, Hall manages a few jibes at nations in the real world.

Hall's is a winning satire, its tone urbane and witty. Mercurius smiles at what he sees, puns villainously, and makes jokes about himself. In Viraginia, for example, he expresses gratitude that his own homeliness makes him unattractive to women, and on his departure from the court of Moronia he breathes a sigh of relief that he is no courtier. Indeed, the sojourn of the Cambridge pilgrim is a long series of comic misadventures, narrow escapes from the entrapments of "monsters," whose leers, vacant stares, and grasping hands represent a world inverted and distorted, as in a funhouse mirror.

Hall's Latin original went through several European editions and was translated into German in 1613. Healey's translation was reprinted in 1613 or 1614, and in a corrupt and pirated edition in 1684. The fullest contemporary estimate was unfortunately that of Milton, who as a religious adversary was as displeased with *Mundus* as he was with its author:

> That grave and noble invention which the greatest and sublimest wits in sundry ages, Plato in *Critias,* and our two famous countrymen, the one in his *Utopia,* the other in his *New Atlantis* chose, I may not say as a field, but as a mighty continent wherein to display the largeness of their spirits by teaching this our world better and exacter things, than were yet known, or used, the petty prevaricator of America, the zanie of Columbus, (for so he must be till his worlds end) having rambled over the huge topography of his own vain thoughts, no marvel, if he brought home nothing but a mere tankard drollery, a venerous parjetory for a stews. Certainly he that could endure with a sober pen to sit and devise laws for drunkards to carouse by, I doubt me whether the very soberness of such a one, like an unliquored Silenus, were not stark drunk.[13]

Hall's caricature is crude, his wit sometimes academic and forced, but Milton's cavils notwithstanding, *Mundus* is a clever satire and in Healey's translation eminently readable. It is also an original satire, for while its mixture of fantasy and mockery recalls Lucian and a few of its details Herodotus, Rabelais, and Erasmus, the main features of the work are his.[14] Indeed, considering how much Hall resembles Swift in his satiric technique it is surprising that modern critics have not made more of *Mundus.* Hall anticipated Swift's use of the outsider as ironic observer, his use of the fantastic voyage as narrative motif, and Hall's Moronia is sufficiently like the grotesque world of Gulliver's third voyage to suggest a possible influence. Moreover, the topsy-turvydom of Hall's Antarctica is an ingenious variation on an ancient theme in European literature, the world upside-down;[15]

and while his world *alter et idem* may have been, as Hall's original editor William Knight averred, "the same as the Platonists dream of," it is to Hall's credit that he could put such doctrine to use as a satiric principle. Certainly, in his fusion of erudition and nonsense, fantasy and caricature, Hall is in the finest tradition of Humanistic satire even if his achievement is somewhat less than that of his great predecessor More, or his great successor, Swift.

For Hall, the end of satire was always a truth deeper than comedy: moral awareness. That was its justification, something Hall always required of his literary enterprises. In satire he found a vent for his Puritanism, a use for his classical learning, and an exercise for his acute eye for social detail—all in the public good. Satire was also a valuable apprenticeship, for in that genre Hall honed his pen for graver studies. But his satire was also literature, and as such it must be judged. Moderns have concurred with ancients in thinking satire a minor genre, and Hall's is not great satire. But it is effective satire, Milton's cavils notwithstanding, for Hall was a good marksman. He knew the contours of his moral, social, and philosophical targets; his arrows found their way home time and time again. To moderns, Hall's caricature is broad, even gross, his wit sometimes indelicate. But Renaissance satire had rules of form and tone; and Hall, like other satirists of his time, was obedient to both. To make folly known, Hall would have argued, it must be painted to life, perhaps even larger than life. This Hall tried to do. If his satires are to be judged as literature they should be judged in the context of Renaissance satire and the formal and material demands of its kind. Later, invested with episcopal dignities, Hall would recall his literary apprenticeship with embarrassment. By then, however, he was master of another medium.

CHAPTER 3

The Taxonomy of Morals

ESTABLISHED at Hawstead, Hall turned moralist, a role for which he was well prepared by education and temperament. Yet his decision to give up the flail for the ferule was neither sudden nor radical. The satirist is always a moralist after a fashion; his business, too, is the critique of values, and although his methods are crude and caustic he shares the moralist's concern for the ethical betterment of his race. The truth is that Hall had long brooded on the foibles and follies of men, and he was now ready to lead them to better ways in literary forms more congenial with his priestly vocation and more apt to gain the attention of persons in high places. Genuinely devout and concerned for the spiritual welfare of his countrymen, he was nonetheless also ambitious. He wanted to rise in the ecclesiastical order, and he knew that to do so he would have to become known beyond the grounds of his parish church. His satires had been directed largely at other university men who could appreciate his classical imitation and academic wit; his new audience would be a broader public, including kings as well as tradesmen, hungry, Hall sincerely believed, for moral instruction. Always conscious that his literary talents were gifts of God, he was anxious to put them to good use.

I   Heaven Upon Earth

Hall's moral philosophy is best expressed in his *Heaven Upon Earth*, a little book published first in 1606, with second and third editons in 1607 and 1609. In his dedication to the Earl of Huntingdon, Hall declares his purpose is "to teach men how to be happy in this life," an aim he was confident he had achieved despite the brevity of his book and the elusiveness of its theme. Hall, as it turned out, had no new formula for happiness; most of his ideas he had got from his reading of classical moralists, St. Augustine, and

43

the Scriptures. But the book is a useful introduction to Hall's moral philosophy and to his prose style; and after the obscurity of the satires it is refreshing to turn to something Hall was at pains to make clear.

Heaven Upon Earth is divided into twenty-seven sections and has a diagrammatic orderliness typical of many learned treatises of the time.[1] The contents of the book may be quickly summarized. Hall begins by defining tranquillity as an emotional equilibrium impervious to depression or lightheartedness but "hanging equal and unmoved betwixt." Finding obstacles to tranquillity in guilt and fear, he methodically analyzes the causes, degrees, and remedies of each, concluding that repentance, faith, and control of the passions will reconcile man to God and to himself and that the anticipation, acceptance, and appreciation of "crosses" (i.e. misfortune) will mitigate the torment of real and imagined fears. He surveys false values such as riches, honors, and pleasures, noting the vanity of each and furnishing historical examples of men caught in such snares, and provides positive rules for peace of mind, enjoins obedience and prayer, and urges the acceptance of one's lot in life.

In composing his treatise, Hall followed Seneca, whose *De Tranquillitate Animi* dealt with the same theme and whose definition of happiness Hall borrowed.[2] The leader of the so-called middle Stoa or Roman School of Stoicism, Seneca had believed in the existence of a god and the soul, had preached the control of the passions and the importance of duty, and, although a heathen, had developed doctrines industrious Christian divines might accommodate to Christian theology, as the Belgian scholar Justus Lipsius had done in attempting to reconcile Stoic determinism with divine providence. In antiquity, Seneca had been praised by Lactantius, St. Jerome, and Tertullian as "our Seneca," and like Cicero had been all but incorporated into the Christian pantheon.[3] Hall's contemporaries held Seneca in hardly less esteem. Although Thomas Lodge's translation of Seneca's moral discourses was not published until 1614, Seneca's nondramatic writing had been read, quoted copiously, and venerated in the Latin original by several generations of Humanist scholars and educated gentlemen.[4] The enormous influence of Seneca's tragedies on Elizabethan and Jacobean drama need not be mentioned.

Hall has been called the "English Seneca" or "Christian Seneca,"[5] usually with the implication that his debt was in principle as well as

style; but it is easy to misconstrue Hall's "Senecanism" even though
he himself was at great pains to define it. The severity of the Stoic
code naturally appealed to Hall, a man of austere personal habits.
But although Hall praised the Stoic philosophers and Seneca in
particular ("never any heathen wrote more divinely, never any
philosopher more probably"), his intention was to supercede those
classical moralists whom he admired for their wisdom but whose
precepts he believed were limited by their dependence on natural
reason. The opening paragraph of *Heaven Upon Earth* makes this
point clearly:

> When I had studiously read over the moral writings of some wise heathen,
> especially those of the Stoical profession, I must confess I found a little envy
> and pity striving together within me: I envied Nature in them, to see her so
> witty in devising such plausible refuges for doubting and troubled minds: I
> pitied them, to see that their careful disquisition of true rest led them, in
> the end, but to mere unquietness. Wherein, methought, they were as
> hounds swift of foot, but not exquisite in scent; which in a hasty pursuit take
> a wrong way, spending their mouths and courses in vain. Their praise of
> guessing wittily they shall not lose; their hopes, both they lost and
> whosoever follows them. (VI, 3)[6]

To Hall, the heathen philosopher might approximate truth, but
never fully grasp it, nor could Stoic resignation ever provide a true
remedy for the ills of fortune: "Not Athens must teach this lesson,
but Jerusalem."

Hall's treatise is, then, in many ways more a critique of Stoic
philosophy (indeed, of reason without revelation) than an endorse-
ment. Hall summarizes Seneca's remedies for an unquiet mind only
to show them insufficient and uses illustrations of heathen fortitude
to prove it futile. We hear echoes of Stoicism in Hall's insistence
that to anticipate pain is to mitigate it, in his disparagement of
honors and riches, and in his conviction of the inconstancy and
unreliability of earthly things; but such ideas are as much Christian
as Stoic. Although like Seneca, Hall was concerned as to how a man
might live happily in a world of flux, his "positive rules" for tranquillity assumed a divine providence and the saving principle of
faith. Friendship, business affairs, public service—the means
Seneca counseled to avoid depression—were to Hall merely a part
of the passing scene. We live here "in an ocean of troubles, wherein
we can see no firm land." Man's only resort is above:

All earthly things are full of variableness, and therefore, having no stay in themselves can give none to us. He that will have and hold right tranquillity must find in himself a sweet fruition of God, and a feeling apprehension of his presence; that when he finds manifold occasions of vexation in these earthly things, he, overlooking them all, and having recourse to his Comforter, may find in Him such matter of contentment, that he may pass over all these petty grievances with contempt; which whosoever wants may be secure, cannot be quiet. (VI, 32)

Hall's reliance on Christian theology is clearly seen in his discussion of the unquiet conscience. Here, Hall takes the reader step by step from the recognition of sin to the realization that there can be no peace without reconciliation, no reconciliation without remission, and no remission with satisfaction, to a meditation on, and celebration of, Christ's redeeming act. Hall's is thus a dark vision of the world—like Seneca's a vision of impending and unavoidable troubles—but it is one that foresees salvation, not dependent as in Stoicism on personal resolution and fortitude, but on the Christian virtues of humility, patience, and faith.

Significantly, Hall was also eager to reject Stoic apathy. Seneca preached salvation in indifference, allowing even suicide in cases of extreme hardship, pain, or disgrace. Finding the world uncertain and mysterious he held misfortune inevitable and encouraged the wise man to ignore it. This characteristically Stoic attitude drew heavy fire in the seventeenth century from Christian divines who insisted that although Christianity and Stoicism shared a contempt for the world, they could not share a disregard for the evil that invited God's providence.[7] The Christian, they argued, must respond positively to suffering, with gratitude and even cheerfulness. Accordingly, Hall declared, "Crosses, unjustly termed evils, as they are sent of him that is all goodness; so they are sent for good, and his end cannot be frustrate." To Hall, Seneca mistook the point of suffering in urging that it be ignored, for from the "crosses" of life the Christian perceives the malady of the soul and the terms of the human condition.

Hall's view of death is yet another indication of his variance from Stoicism. Seneca had dealt with the fear of death in several of his moral epistles. In *On Despising Death,* for example, he gave instances of famous persons who had faced death unafraid, who had "despised that moment when the soul breathes its last."[8] Hall, on the other hand, dwells on the horrors of death to show them no illusion but a horrible reality and extends the anguish of dying into the eternal world. "If our momentary sufferings seem long, how long shall that be that is eternal." He also cites examples, not of heroic indifference but of awful suffering, and the prospect he holds out for relief from terror is not resignation to the inevitable but the prospect of heaven. "The Epicure or Sadduccee dare not die, for fear of not being; the guilty and the loose worldling dares not die, because he knows not whether he shall be miserable or not be at all; the resolved Christian dares and would die, because he knows he shall be happy."

Although full of doctrine, *Heaven Upon Earth* is not dull reading, and it is easy to see why it might have been popular. Hall is variously ironic, witty, and dramatic—he shows flashes of humor, despite the overall somberness of his world view, although his humor is of a sardonic sort. We are often reminded, in reading the treatise, of Hall the satirist, for to Hall it is not enough that the recalcitrant worldling be proven wrong; he must also be shown absurd. "The drunken man is as thirsty as the sweating traveller," he observes. "The man of nice education hath a feeble stomach, and, rasping since his last meal, doubts whether he should eat of his best dish or nothing." Homely adages such as these—the *exempla* of Hall's precepts—anticipate the categorization and neatly filed *sententiae* of his *Characters:*

The mind of man cannot want some refuge; and, as we say of the elephant, cannot rest, unless it have something to lean upon. The covetous man, whose heaven is his chest, when he hears himself rated and cursed for oppressions, comes home, and seeing his bags safe, applauds himself against all censures. The glutton, when he loseth friends or good name, yet joyeth in his well furnished table and the laughter of his wine; more pleasing himself in one dish than he can be grieved with all the world's miscarriage. The needy scholar, whose wealth lies all in his brain, cheers himself against iniquity of times with the conceit of his knowledge. (VI, 32–3)

A dissonance for the modern reader is Hall's persistent note of self-congratulation. He is very sure of his doctrine, and of himself, contemptuous of those outside the pale of his orthodoxy. Charity moves him to write, and yet sharing Seneca's view that the world is full of fools, he treats his readers as potential adversaries. While he is willing to warn the wordly-minded of their sinful ways, like Jonah he is a somewhat reluctant prophet. Let the Devil take his own, he seems to say, concluding the treatise with an invitation to the hard of heart to persist in their vanities.

II   Characters

The best known of Hall's moral writings are his *Characters of Vertues and Vices* (1608), twenty-four prose essays modeled on the *Ethical Characters* of Theophrastus. There were English precedents for character writing in the personified seven deadly sins of medieval allegory and in the thumbnail sketch of moral and social types often found in the Elizabethan sermon and pamphlet, but a book composed wholly of such portraiture was a novelty in seventeenth-century England.[9]

Although Hall thought his *Characters* original, he believed "charactery" to be a traditional art. In a preface to the volume—"A Premonition of the Title and Use of Characters"—he identified himself with that class of moral philosopher who of old combined precept and example in "speaking pictures, or lively images." By such means, Hall explained, "the ruder multitude might, even by their sense, learn to know virtue, and to discern what to detest." In "charactery" Hall believed he had found a mode of instruction that might, without exhortation or dissuasion, heighten the moral awareness of his readers.

In composing characters, Hall followed an "ancient master of morality," the Greek philosopher Theophrastus, whose *Ethical Characters* consisted of thirty-two sketches of social "types." The Theophrastan characters were satirical in tone, and although presented as moral instruction in a preface (almost surely by another hand in a later age), they seem designed largely to amuse. Hall broadened the scope and altered the emphasis of his model by characterizing virtue as well as vice and by infusing his characters with his own particular moral bias: the Christian Stoicism of his *Heaven Upon Earth*. He also gave the character a more definite form. The Theophrastan sketch began with a definition and concluded with a series of illustrative vignettes, all within the compass of a few hundred words. Hall's characters are more fully developed, begin with a definition of a moral quality or description of its possessor, proceed to lower levels of generality through a combination of vignette and *sententiae*, and conclude, emphatically, with a volley of terse epithets.

Hall's *Characters* exemplify a severe moral typology. When he tells us in his "proem" to Book I that "virtue is not loved, because she is not seen; and vice loseth much detestation, because her ugliness is a secret," he is telling us both that experience is illusory and moral reality simple. There is virtue and there is vice. Within that conceptual frame, all morality is comprehended. The key to recognition is the eye, for Hall shared Plato's notion that morals and aesthetics were related. If we fail to see Vice for what it is, our misunderstanding does not make Vice a Virtue. We, rather, are "blind and bewitched" by the world, which conceals the beauty of virtue and the foulness of vice.

Although behind this construct is the traditionally Christian dualism of good vs. evil, there is also Hall's training as a rhetorician. Praise and blame—long identified with virtue and vice—were central motives in the academic exercises of his time. George Puttenham in his *Arte of English Poesie* had placed the "character" among epideictic types, the discourse of praise and blame.[10] Hall's moral taxonomy also suggests the dichotomizing tendency of Ramist logic. Hall's two-part division of morals was thus compatible with both the traditional dualism of Christian ethics and one of the more fashionable intellectual perspectives of his time.

In his *Characters of Vertues* Hall treats eleven qualities: Wisdom, Honesty, Faithfulness, Humility, Valiancy, Patience, True Friendship, True Nobility, Justice, Penitence, and Happiness. His treatment of each represents a conflation of classical and Christian moral ideals: his Faithful Man, Humble Man, and Penitent obviously owe much to the theology and imagery of St. Paul; the Valiant Man, the Truly Noble and the True Friend reveal his classical reading. Dominant throughout are the Stoic themes of self-knowledge, self-control and self-sufficiency. In all his Characters, however, Hall strives to make something of Christian piety. As a consequence, even Hall's Wise Man, whom Hall represents as a skilled logician—"his working mind doth nothing all his time but make syllogisms and draw out conclusions"—seeks first the state of his soul, and his Truly Noble "is more careful to give true honor to his Maker, than to receive civil honour from men." It may therefore be said that although some of Hall's virtues are those of a virtuous heathen, all are the proper goal of good Christians.

Hall's character of the Wise Man may serve further as an example of Hall's intellectual ideals as well as his practical bent. Although like Bacon, Hall's Wise Man takes all knowledge for his province ("There is nothing that he desires not to know"), that knowledge he desires most is of the self, which he attains by close observation of men and things, a turning of observation to precept and precept to practice. Thus, the end of his wisdom is not to speak but to act and to learn before himself presuming to teach others. Hall's Wise Man is chiefly an observer rather than a reader, although that he is the latter as well is implied in Hall's insistence that the Wise Man can understand the present and predict the future because he knows the past. He minds his own business, is an excellent teacher, and his wisdom manifests itself in his self-control ("His passions are so many good servants, which stand in a diligent attendance, ready to be commanded by reason, by religion"), and in his steadfastness. For although he is marvellously alert to the passing scene, he remains aloof from it. "He stands like a centre, unmoved, while the circumference of his estate is drawn above, beneath, about him." Significantly Hall's Wise Man is very much in this world, even if he may not be of it; for although wisdom for Hall begins in a logical operation, its proof is in knowing how to deploy one's energies for the greatest good of the self and others.

Of Hall's "virtues," only one is represented by a social role: The Good Magistrate. Here Hall's intent seems not to have been the mere personification of Justice, but an outline of the moral obligations of the Elizabethan civil servant, who was in his office both judge and administrator. The provenance of Hall's ideas in this character is the Elizabethan political commonplace, which viewed magistracy as a pivotal link in that "great chain of being" extending from God above to the beasts below.[11] Yet although Hall goes so far as to call the Magistrate "another God on earth," he is careful to emphasize the social responsibilities of the Good Magistrate. "His nights, his meals are short and interrupted; all which he bears well, because he knows himself made for a public servant of peace and justice. . . .On the bench he is another from himself at home; now all private respects, of blood, alliance, amity, are forgotten." For Hall, the magistrate's office requires an even stricter code than that exacted from the ordinary Christian: "Pity, the best praise of Humanity and the fruit of Christian love," is checked. A rugged forehead and severe countenance become standard equipment in the war against vice and villainy.

Hall's Happy Man was one of two characters added to the edition of 1615, probably to round out his gallery of virtues with the depiction of a man possessing them all, for although Hall's "happiness" is more virtue rewarded than a virtue itself, the character comes closest to describing Hall's ideal: the perfect integration of Stoic and Christian virtues. It is easy, however, to overestimate the Stoic influence in this character. The Happy Man knows himself, is indifferent to poverty or wealth, "lives quietly at home, out of the noise of the world; and loves to enjoy himself always; and sometimes his friends; and hath as full scope to his thoughts as to his eyes." He has a healthy mind in a healthy body, an even temper, and an independent spirit. All might have been drawn from Seneca's *De Tranquillitate* alone, had Hall not so completely absorbed the Stoic ethic making that kind of imitation unnecessary. But Hall's Happy Man is his whole moral philosophy in microcosm. Senecan integrity secures peace in this life, but what of the world to come? In this character, the Happy Man's Christian devotion is placed climactically to suggest both its indispensibility and its superiority to the virtues of Stoic morality. For Hall, the most perfect happiness of the Happy Man lies in the illumination and exaltation of mystical experience:

> His soul is every day dilated to receive that God in whom he is; and hath attained to love himself for God, and God for his own sake. His eyes stick so fast in heaven, that no earthly object can remove them: yea, his whole self is there before his time; and sees with Stephen, and hears with Paul, and enjoys with Lazarus, the glory that he shall have; and takes possession beforehand of his room amongst the saints. And these heavenly contentments have so taken him up, that now he looks down displeasedly upon the earth, as the region of his sorrow and banishment. (VI, 105)

There are more characters of Vice than of Virtue, perhaps because Hall thought Vice capable of more variety. In any case, in his "vices" Hall followed Theophrastus in featuring social types. Some, like the Busy-Body, the Superstitious, and the Malcontent have Theophrastan counterparts which may have suggested some details in Hall's portraits. In all, however, Hall's debt to Theophrastus has been overstated. It is the vice of scholars to think every correspondence a debt and to demand of every observation its "source." Hall, however, did not need to read Theophrastus to know ambition, flattery, laziness, or vainglory when he saw them. As a keen observer of men, a frequenter of court and town, he was aware of the vagaries of human nature.

Unlike Theophrastus, whose portraiture is genial satire, Hall saw vice as a deformity; and his vices personified are all social misfits, inimical to the best interests of themselves and their neighbors and hostile to reason and religion. Wisdom leads Hall's virtues because she presupposes them all; similarly, Hall places Hypocrisy first among the evils because "she cometh nearest to virtue and is the worst of vices." Busy-Body follows the Hypocrite, perhaps because he hides his nosiness under a "pretense of love" and is therefore a hypocrite of a lesser order. The Superstitious and the Profane are in sequence to contrast the credulity of one with the atheism of the other. Elsewhere, Hall's arrangement seems random, and there is no clear effort to provide among the "vices" direct counterparts for Hall's "virtues." What Hall did intend was that the reader mark the contrast between the two books of the *Characters:* life lived according to reason and religion as opposed to life lived sinfully and foolishly. That Hall planned so to structure the reader's experience of the *Characters* is suggested in his "Proem" to Book II:

I have showed you many fair virtues. I speak not for them: if their sight cannot command affection, let them lose it. They shall please yet better after you have troubled your eyes a little with the view of deformities; and by how much more they please, so much more odious and like themselves shall these deformities appear. This light contraries gives to each other in the midst of their enmity, that one makes the other seem more good or ill. (VI, 106)

Hall's *Characters* has been called static and colorless,[12] and there is some justification for this criticism in the *Characters of Vertues* where Hall's theme obliged him to follow a decorum of high seriousness. All this changes in Hall's "vices," however. In his "Proem" to Book II he further observes that his portraits of vice might "seem less grave, more satirical," a shift in tone he attributed to the fact that some "evils are, besides the odiousness, ridiculous."

A main strategy in Hall's *Characters of Vices* is the satirical vignette: the miniature drama in which a vice manifests itself in the social behavior of its possessor. An example is this scene from Hall's Hypocrite:

Walking early up into the city, he turns into the great church, and salutes one of the pillars on one knee; worshipping that God, which at home he cares not for: while his eye is fixed on some window, on some passenger;

and his heart knows not whither his lips go: he rises, and, looking about with admiration, complains of our frozen charity; commends the ancient. At church he will ever sit where he may be seen best; and in the midst of the sermon pulls out his tables in haste, as if he feared to lose that note; when he writes, either his forgotten errand, or nothing: then he turns his Bible with a noise to seek an omitted quotation; and folds the leaf, as if he had found it; and asks aloud the name of the preacher, and repeats it; whom he publicly salutes, thanks, praises, invites, entertains with tedious good coun sel, with good discourse, if it had come from an honester mouth. (VI, 107)

Here Hall captures hypocrisy in a bit of droll comedy he must have seen enacted a dozen times both in St. Paul's, London, and in his own parish church. The concrete detail, the careful limning of the Hypocrite's calculated postures, gives the vignette a psychological authenticity as well as a humorous effect.

Similar qualities are evident in this scene from the Busy-Body:

If he see but two men talk, and read a letter in the street, he runs to them, and asks if he may not be partner of that secret relation; and if they deny it, he offers to tell, since he may not hear, wonders: and then falls upon the report of the Scottish mine, or the great fish taken up at Lynn, or of the freezing of the Thames and, after many thanks and dismissions, is hardly entreated silence. (VI, 108)

It is Hall's sense of the ridiculous that for modern readers saves his "vices" from the colorlessness of his "virtues." In his character of the Superstitious, for example, Hall successfully recreates the whole psychological ambience of the man who feels himself constantly vulnerable to supernatural menace:

This man dares not stir forth till his breast be crossed and his face sprinkled. If but an hare cross him in the way, he returns; or if his journey began, unawares, on the dismal day; or, if he stumbled at the threshold. If he see a snake unkilled, he fears mischief; if the salt fall toward him, he looks pale and red, and is not quiet till one of the waiters have poured wine on his lap; and when he sneezeth, thinks them not his friends that uncover not. (VI, 109)

Equally comic and satiric are Hall's descriptions of the Covetous Man returning to his cottage enraged to know "what became of the loose crust in his cupboard, and who hath rioted amongst his leeks." Or the account of the fantastic posturing of the courtier (The Vainglorious), who pretends to have letters, actually composed by himself, from persons of high station inviting him to dine.

What Hall's "vices" provide is the feel of life, a mis-en-scène of concrete details, gestures, topical allusions, folklore and motives which are, though base, cruel, or ridiculous, thoroughly human and perennial. We have almost returned to the world of Hall's satires, with its leering faces, crowded streets, and atmosphere of moral decay. Not to be overlooked is Hall's ability to capture the essence of folly in a trenchant phrase. Of the Malcontent he observes with mock sonority, "In the deep silence of the night, the very moonshine openeth his clamorous mouth." He finds the Flatterer's whole design to "make men fools in teaching them to overvalue themselves and to tickle his friends to death." The Unconstant Man is a "guest in his own house"; the Vainglorious, "A Spanish soldier on an Italian theatre"; the Envious, "a lean and pale carcass quickened with a fiend." And he concludes of the Hypocrite that he is "a rotten stick in the dark night," and affirms the Slothful "witty in nothing but framing excuses to sit still."

Posthumously, Sir Thomas Overbury paid Hall the compliment of imitation in 1614 in the second printing of a poem, A Wife, to which were added twenty-one characters by Overbury and other hands, including John Webster and John Donne. These "Characters," following Hall's in form but without his moral purpose, emphasize realistic background and coarse comic detail. Nicholas Breton published his Characters Upon Essays Moral and Divine the year following but treated qualities or states without personifying them. Breton's Characters shows the relationship of character-writing to the still nascent essay form. The last significant collection of the period was that of John Earle, whose Microcosmography contained over fifty sketches in the first edition of genial and philosophical portraiture, like the Overburian characters, without strong didactic emphasis. As Boyce suggests, while Hall pioneered the form, the Overburians set the example for content in later character writers.[13] Yet Hall's Characters has always had readers and admirers. His was one of the first—if not the first—English books to be translated into French, and from the French it was translated into German at least four times during the seventeenth century.[14]

III   Epistles

As a letter writer, Hall had his English predecessors, despite his claim in the preface to *Epistles* (3 vols., 1608–11) that they represented a "new fashion of discourse, new to our language." William Fulwood and Abraham Fleming had published "epistles" in 1568 and 1576, respectively; and Angel Day's *The English Secretorie* informed Elizabethans concerning the form and proper matter of "epistles and familiar letters" as early as 1586. But the letters of Fulwood and Fleming were largely translations from classical authors; and Day's *Secretorie*, while containing some sample epistles, was finally only a handbook based on classical rhetoric. Hall's *Epistles* were the first English letters to stand comparison with those of the Latin masters, Cicero, Pliny, and Seneca.

Hall's epistles were arranged in six "decades" or units of ten letters each and addressed to friends, patrons, and lords and ladies of the court of Prince Henry, whom Hall served as chaplain until the Prince's death in 1612. They provide a glimpse, therefore, of the life of the age, at least as perceived by a cleric of austere personal habits and moralizing temper. Although the epistles are undated, allusions to events private and public suggest many were no sooner composed than sent off to the printer. Most seem to have been actual correspondence; all were obviously written or revised with an eye to publication.

Renaissance guides to letter writing usually treated the epistle as a kind of oration.[15] Hall thought it, rather, a colloquial and familiar form in which "we do but talk with our friends by our pen and express ourselves no whit less easily, somewhat more digestedly." But while Hall's epistles are not orations, neither are they "familiar" in our modern sense. They contain little news, the idiom is formal, and each is titled and tightly organized around a theme.

In his conception of epistolary style Hall followed Erasmus, Lipsius, and the example of Seneca, whose *Epistulae Morales* were much prized by English Humanists and whose epistles, as Bacon had observed, were really little essays. Erasmus in his *Modus Conscribiendi Epistolis* defined the epistle as a conversation between absent friends, a definition Angel Day borrowed in his English *Secretorie*. Lipsius, chief Renaissance expositor of Seneca, defined the qualities of the epistle as brevity, perspicuity, simplicity, charm *(venustas)*, and propriety *(decencia)*, principles to which Hall adhered in his view that the epistle should be "more free, more familiar" and in his belief that brevity made instruction more memorable:

I grant that brevity, where it is neither obscure not defective, is very pleasing, even to the daintiest judgments. No marvel, therefore, if most men desire much good counsel in a narrow room; as some affect to have great personages drawn in little tablets; or, as we see worlds of countries described in the compass of small maps. Neither do I unwillingly yield to follow them: for both the powers of good advice are the stronger when they are thus united; and brevity makes counsel more portable for memory, and readier for use. (VI, 311)

Some of Hall's themes are Senecan, and his epistles follow a format similar to that of the Roman moralist's: an initial allusion to a specific event in Hall or his correspondent's life, then general reflection on some moral issue, expressed tersely and impersonally in *sententiae* and proverb. As usual, however, Hall's imitation is far from slavish.

Although arranged randomly, Hall's epistles tend to be of three sorts: moral, doctrinal, or polemical. Epistles of the first category treat commonplace Renaissance themes with arguments Hall had from his reading of classical authors. They exhort, commend, console; but the degree to which the nominal correspondent shapes Hall's manner or matter varies from letter to letter. Some of the moral epistles deal with traditional subjects. The letters to Lord Hay ("Of True Honor"), Matthew Milward ("On the Pleasure of Study and Contemplation"), and Sir Andrew Asteley ("On our due Preparation for Death") make little or no reference to the addressee and might properly have been sent to anyone. "On the Benefit of retirement and secrecy," composed for Sir Edmund Bacon, Hall's former patron and traveling companion, is warm and congratulatory, but while making specific allusions to Bacon's career and private habits, includes much in the oracular manner of Sir Francis Bacon's essays:

For great places have seldom safe and easy entrances; and, which is worse, great charges can hardly be plausibly wielded without some indirect policies. Alas! their privileges cannot countervail their toil. Weary days and restless nights, short lives and long cares, weak bodies and unquiet minds, attend lightly on greatness: either clients break their sleep in the morning, or the intention of their mind drives it off from the first watch: either suits or complaints thrust themselves into their recreations, and packets of letters interrupt their meals: it is ever term with them, without vacation: their businesses admit no night, no holiday. (VI, 160)

It was the moral content of his epistles that relieved Hall from the charge of vanity in publishing his correspondence. Convinced that instruction was a kind of pleasure, he did not fail to please in the way suited to his learning, temperament, and priestly vocation. But not all the moral epistles are tissues of commonplaces. In letters of consolation, for example, he often shows a logical rigor and ingenuity of the kind John Donne had made fashionable in his funeral verses. To "J. B." ("Against the Fear of Death"), Hall demonstrates the unreasonableness of fearing death by showing that it is a necessary adjunct of life:[16] "Think, that death is necessarily annexed to nature. We are for a time on condition that we shall not be; we receive life but upon terms of redelivery. Necessity makes some things easy, as it usually makes easy things difficult. It is a fond injustice to embrace the covenant and shrink at the condition" (VI, 157). To "W. R." ("Consolations of Immoderate grief for the death of friends"), Hall consoles the bereaved husband and father with a witty justification of grief:

> You had but two jewels, which you held precious; a wife and a son: one was yourself divided; the other, yourself multiplied: you have lost both, and well-near at once. The loss of one caused the loss of the other, and both of them your just grief. Such losses, when they come single, afflict us; but when double, astonish us: and though they give advantage of respite, would almost overwhelm the best patient. (VI, 180)

And in his epistle to I. A. Merchant ("Against Sorrow for Worldly losses") he argues for the blessings "of a mean estate" in such a way as to suggest that he had forgotten nothing of his early training as a rhetorician:

> The fear of some evils is worse than the sense. To speak ingenuously; I could never see wherein poverty deserved so hard a conceit. It takes away the delicacy of fare, softness of lodging, gayness of attire; and, perhaps, brings with it contempt: this is the worst, and all. View it now on the better side: lo there, quiet security, sound sleeps, sharp appetite, free merriment; no fears, no cares, no suspicion, no distempers of excess, no discontentment. If I were judge, my tongue should be unjust if poverty went away weeping. I cannot see how the evils it brings can compare with those which it removes; how the discommodities should match the blessings of the mean estate. (VI, 183–4)

Most of Hall's letters are either doctrinal or polemic. They treat the moral requirements of the Christian life, resolve sticky ethical questions, or assail his religious opponents. The letters enjoining Christian piety (e.g. To Mr. Robert Hay, "Of the continual exercise of a Christian; how he may keep his heart from hardness and his ways from error") are bland sermons, full of good counsel tersely expressed. The casuistical pieces are more interesting, not because moderns share Hall's views on divorce, adultery, sexual abstinence among husband and wife, or commerce between Christian and infidel, but because Hall's deliberations suggest what a learned man of his age might consider morally lawful. The polemical epistles are much in the fashion of the time: bold, rancorous, conceited. Hall's epistles "On the marriage of ecclesiastical persons" is a miniature thesis defending the clergy's right to marry. A letter to Sir David Murray is a cynical analysis of Roman "miracles," in which Hall concludes that "all popish miracles are either falsely reported, or falsely done, or falsely miraculous, or falsely ascribed to Heaven" (VI, 148). Of special interest is Hall's epistle to John Smith and John Robinson, leaders of the Separatists and founders of the Plymouth Colony. Hall's epistle is censorious, and he has been criticized by one biographer for his presumption in attacking the founders of a great nation.[17] But while it is true that Hall minces few words in dealing with the Separatists—"in setting forth their injury done to the .Church, the injustice of their cause, and fearfulness of their offence," Hall would have condemned the self-imposed exile of the Pilgrim fathers even had he forseen its consequences. Hall feared and hated nothing more than schism. It was hostile to his own accommodating and compromising nature and incompatible with that "middle ground" on which he felt the English Reformed Church to be justly situated. To Hall, the Separatists were guilty of deserting the Church and the nation in a time of need and of over-emphasizing the importance of ritual, which to Hall was "for ornament more than use; not parts of the building, but not necessary appendances." His epistle, therefore, while avoiding personal attacks against Robinson and Smith, does not hesitate to denounce their separation as moral error, dangerous to themselves and to others in the example.

Hall's *Epistles* typify his moral writings. The personality of the sober churchman infuses every page, reflecting his reverence for order, tradition, and inherited wisdom. A few of the epistles provide glimpses into Hall's private life, his travels, and his daily routine of study, meditation, and ministry. But even these allusions are made to do service as exempla, and most of the epistles express what was often (in Hall's age) thought but never previously expressed with so admirable a terseness and polish. Moderns suffocating in Hall's moral earnestness may wonder why Hall thought his epistles entertaining as well as instructive. The answer, of course, is that Hall's age did find instruction entertaining, tradition comforting, eloquence trustworthy. Hall's moral writings were popular, as their frequent editions suggest, and they earned Hall respect both as an author and as a man. Like his satires and characters, the *Epistles* became a model for later writers, who handled the form with more wit but perhaps less moral earnestness. For all the inadequacies of Hall's letters, they justify his status as a pioneer in English literature.

IV   *Cases of Conscience*

To Hall, the most useful branch of divinity was that dealing with cases of conscience; but although, as we have seen, a number of his epistles are casuistical, his chief work of this sort was *Resolutions and Decisions of Divers Practical Cases of Conscience*, published in 1648. This book, tendered as "probable advices for the simpler sort of Christians," consists of four decades treating, respectively, the ethics of business, civic responsibility, religion, and matrimony. In each "case," Hall's method is to pose a question, answer it with a general principle, and explore the issue to discover possible objections, exceptions, or qualifications. The basis of his judgment is as always Holy Scripture, and sometimes natural law, a principle he seems to have identified with what was instinctual and universal in man. The cases themselves are replete with allusions to his classical reading and to the work of contemporary Roman and Reformed casuists, but his manner is to resolve in favor of Christian charity where he found no warrant in Scripture or in nature.

Hall's views of the morality of business enterprises confirm the impression given in his verse satires that he had both a strong distaste for economic injustice and a good working knowledge of economics. He condemns usury, profiteering, unauthorized monopolies and supports price controls; but in determining business ethics he is concerned with motivation, and his governing principle is a concern for one's neighbor, noting that "in all human and civil acts of commerce it is a sure rule, that whatsoever is not a violation of charity cannot be unlawful; and whatsoever is not agreeable to charity can be no other than sinful" (VII, 274). In turning to questions of civil responsibility, Hall is careful to distinguish between the legal and moral aspects of an action, leaving the former to the jurists. It is lawful for one man to kill another in self-defense, he concludes, because self-preservation is a natural instinct; duelling, on the other hand, he condemns as wicked and damnable since it tempts God to preserve the life of the wronged party and constitutes murder by mutual consent. His opinions of suicide and abortion are what we should have supposed: the one is condemned without exception, Hall's admiration for Roman Stoicism notwithstanding; the second is condemned with but one exception, when incidental to an attempt to save both the life of the mother and the unborn child. His views on imperialism ("Whether it be lawful for Christians, where they find a country possessed by savage pagans and infidels, to drive out the native inhabitants, and to seize and enjoy their lands upon any pretence") are more reasonable than we should have expected in an age of rampant colonizing:

Dominion and property is not founded in religion, but in natural and civil right. It is true that the saints have in Christ, the Lord of all things, a spiritual right in all creatures . . . but the spiritual right gives a man no title at all to any natural or civil possession here on earth. Yet, Christ himself, though both as God and as Mediator the whole world were his; yet he tells Pilate, *My Kingdom is not of this World:* neither did he, though the Lord paramount of this whole earth, by virtue of that transcendent sovereignty, put any man out of the possession of one foot of ground which fell to him either by birth or purchase. Neither doth the want of that spiritual interest debar any man from rightful claim and fruition of these earthly inheritances. (VII, 349–50)

Hall's views on matrimony, dealing as they do largely with definitions of incest and occasions for divorce and annulment, are not quite as interesting as his economic and political opinions: for the most part he simply argues the Scriptural warrant behind the civil code. There is one exception, however; and that is the second case of the fourth decade, in which Hall argues the evil of divorce for any cause other than adultery and makes an unmistakable reference to John Milton's *Doctrine and Discipline of Divorce.* Hall's quarrel with Milton will be discussed at some length in a subsequent chap-

ter; it is enough to say here that their mutual animosity was of long
standing, and nothing could have offended Bishop Hall's conservative moral philosophy more than the social radicalism of the Puritan
poet:

I have heard too much of, and once saw a licentious pamphlet thrown
abroad in these lawless times, in the defence and encouragement of di-
vorces (not to be sued out: that solemnity needed not, but) to be arbitrarily
given by the disliking husband to his displeasing and unquiet wife; upon
this ground, principally, that marriage was instituted for the help and comfort of man: where, therefore the match proves such as that the wife doth
but pull down a side, and by her innate peevishness, and either sullen or
pettish and froward disposition, brings rather discomfort to her husband;
the end of marriage being hereby frustrate, why should it not, saith he, be
in the husband's power, after some prevailing means of reclamation attempted, to procure his own peace by casting off this clog; and to provide for his
own peace and contentment in a fitter match?

Woe is me! to what a pass is the world come, that a Christian, pretending
to reformation, should dare to tender so loose a project to the public! I must
seriously profess, when I first did cast my eye upon the front of the book, I
supposed some great wit meant to try his skill in the maintenance of this so
wild and improbable paradox; but ere I could have run over some of those
too well penned pages, I found the author was in earnest; and meant seriously to contribute this piece of good counsel, in way of reformation, to the
wise and seasonable care of superiors. (VII, 371)

Hall, of course, was happier than Milton in his marriage choices,
but that does not begin to explain the difference in their opinions.
The truth is that Hall could not consider the individual conscience
and its perplexities apart from the larger polemical context; and if he
was angered at Milton's impious departure from traditional Biblical
teaching, he was no less offended by Roman casuists, who, as he
frequently points out in *Cases of Conscience,* encourage license by
sustaining newfangled practices of the Roman pontiff. Hall saw himself in the midst of a lawless age and called to defend divine and
natural law against apostasy and vice. His *Cases,* therefore, while
humbly tendered to the English public, were nonetheless authoritative for faithful Anglicans.

V   *Senecan Style*

Hall came by the title of "The English Seneca" as much for his
style as for his Christian Stoicism.[18] His terse, symmetrical periods,

"hopping short in the measure of convulsion fits,"[19] as Milton complained, deserve a chapter in the history of taste as well as a prominent place in the history of English prose; for like Bacon, Hall was a leader of the anti-Ciceronian movement in the early seventeenth century.

In the sixteenth century Cicero had been the great exemplar of prose style in Latin and in vernacular tongues that aspired to Latin elegance. Schoolboys read, memorized, and "copied" him; scholars redeemed his paganism by imagining his conversion to Christianity or his correspondence with St. Paul. Indeed it is not too much to say that for the Renaissance Cicero was to eloquence what Aristotle was to wisdom: its very embodiment. The métier of Ciceronianism was the periodic sentence, swelling to a climax on waves of subordinate clauses and figures of sound. It was a style that valued *copia* or artful elaboration, circumlocution, and grand effects; but it was a style difficult to imitate, perhaps impossible to master, in English, although it had had by Hall's time distinguished practitioners in Roger Ascham and Richard Hooker.

The revolt against Ciceronian imitation began in the last half of the sixteenth century when Montaigne, scorning Cicero's artificiality, made the blunt, conversational manner of his *Essais* a part of his philosophical program.[20] Even more influential perhaps was the Belgian Humanist Justus Lipsius. An erstwhile Ciceronian, Lipsius in his middle years rejected the manner of the Roman orator, adopted Seneca as his guide, and established brevity as a new fashion in a series of academic discourses, epistles and in an edition of Seneca that became standard. In England, Bacon echoed the call for "Attic" plainness. Although his censure of Ciceronianism as a "delicate and polished kind of learning"[21] was anticipated by his countrymen Thomas Nashe and Gabriel Harvey, Bacon's reputation as a statesman and philosopher made his call for a new prose style all the more authoritative. By the end of the first decade of the seventeenth century, Senecan concinnity was well on its way to replacing Ciceronian grandeur as a model of stylistic excellence.

The distinction between Ciceronian and Senecan styles was largely the distinction anciently made between the *genus grande* and *genus humile*.[22] The first was the language of oratory, valuing variety in repetition, sonority, and ornament; the second, the language of discussion or conversation, prizing brevity, wit, and plainness. As Bacon's censure implied, the distinction was of more than literary importance; for the controversy between the proponents of one *genus* and the other harkened back to the old quarrel between rhetoric and philosophy reflected in Plato's attack on the sophists in the *Phaedrus* and *Gorgias*. There Plato, through his mouthpieces Socrates and the Elean Stranger, had scorned the teaching of eloquence as a miseducation of youth, in that it taught them to prefer appearances to realities. Eloquence, he said, was like cosmetics or cookery it was a knack, no true science. Later authorities, Aristotle for example, put a more favorable construction on rhetoric and on ornate style, but so-called fancy writing has always labored under the charge that it is concealing either something disreputable or nothing at all. That it concealed the latter was Bacon's argument. The example of Seneca provided him with a philosophical language, an idiom in which to express his intellectual curiosity, his skepticism, and to express his wisdom in neatly formulated utterances. Of a less critical spirit, and perhaps under the influence of Ramism which favored a plain over an ornate style,[23] Hall also chose the Stoic model as his guide.

Although there were varieties of Senecanism (Hall and Bacon do not write exactly alike), those varieties shared qualities that make it possible for us to consider them a single stylistic tendency. Most conspicuous of these is the "curt" period or sentence. Hall's sentences rarely exceed over a dozen or so words and, when longer, are generally composed of short clauses or phrases so that the effect of brevity is preserved even when the sentence exceeds the normal range. Hall is fond of colons and semicolons, abrupt transitions, milk-train rhythms and staccato effects; and like other writers of the anti-Ciceronian movement, his preference for such features occasionally leads him beyond succinctness into obscurity, although of this flaw he is much less guilty than other Senecan stylists. Another feature of Hall's sentences is their symmetry. The sententiousness that the seventeenth century admired depended not merely on memorable brevity but memorable structure, and although a plain style, Senecanism retained a number of stylistic devices to give sentences form and polish. Notable among these were isocolon (members of like length) and parison (members of like form), devices Hall used extensively to achieve balance and antithesis. In this sentence from Hall's *Characters*, for example, he displays his love of parallelism as well as his knack for compression: "He had rather complain than offend; and hates sin more for the indignity of it than the danger." Here the words "complain" and "offend," "indignity" and "danger" play off against each other, underscoring the contrast between the honest man and the extraordinary man. The double predication partially conceals the compound structure of the sentence; but the internal punctuation, like a fulcrum, rhetorically equates the balanced members. Notable here is Hall's refusal to reinforce antithesis with like sounds, a common technique of Euphuism and even of Seneca himself. Like Bacon, however, Hall rejected the jingling effect of the figures of sound, preferring parallelism only when useful to reinforce meaning.

Hall's language is plain, his vocabulary simple. Although a skilled Latinist, his diction possesses the vigor of the native idiom, and although learned, he is not ostentatiously so. Hall's writing is rich in simile and metaphor, but these are generally drawn from familiar sources, the habits of beasts, the details of alchemy and agriculture, commerce and warfare, geographic exploration and politics, the furniture of court, household and sanctuary. Preeminent are images drawn from Scripture—the heroic figures of the Patriarchs, the imagery of the Psalms, and the parables of Jesus. All these, of course, are the common property of his age; yet moderns, fresh from a reading of Andrewes or Donne, will find Hall's metaphors ordinary, even trite. There is no straining after effect in Hall. His comparisons are always clearly labeled, his meaning is always plain. Yet if rarely striking, Hall's metaphors are often remarkable for their aptness, as when in his *Characters* he likens the Busy-Body's tongue to the tail of Samson's foxes (VI, 108) or in the *Epistles* when he compares his supicions of the sensuous as "fearing a serpent in that apple" (VI, 282).

The flaw in Hall's method is the inevitable one in any mannered style. At worst, his curt periods seem but a mechanical application of a rhetorical principle, as cultish in its own way as the Ciceronianism it rejected. It is hard, however, to accept Morris Croll's judgment that Hall's style was defective.[24] He was not, ultimately, a littérateur, but a teacher whose passion was moral instruction. If Hall's prose sometimes seems formulaic, it is always serviceable to his ethical program. His terse periods were easily comprehended, readily recollected. The imagery of his prose—the staples of proverb, Scripture, and everyday experience—were congenial to every Englishman's observations, and the content of his aphorisms answered to what his contemporaries felt was eternally true and universally accepted. As a style, Hall's Senecanism was flexible enough to accommodate the varied tones of his didacticism; he could exhort, satirize, compliment, and—as we shall later see—meditate in a single rhetorical idiom.

Finally, Hall's style, like the moral philosophy it expressed, shows him to be in the intellectual mainstream of his time. It was the style of the hour, and its rhetorical austerity permanently displaced Ciceronian opulence. Hall's thought too was timely. The Jacobean court with its amorous intrigues and political scandal could not answer to Hall's exacting code; but it would have recognized it and, hypocritically, applauded it. By providing "much good counsel in a narrow room," he became, like the pagan philosopher he both admired and pitied, the moral preceptor to his generation.

CHAPTER 4

A Somber Muse

HALL wrote some nonsatirical poetry: a handful of occasional poems, "metaphrases" of the Psalms, and three anthems. The occasional verse was written during the first decade of the seventeenth century when Hall was eager for public recognition and when young men of intellectual ability and literary skill were expected to write poems commemorating public events, to festoon the literary efforts of their friends with laudatory prefaces, or to contribute funeral verses on the death of princes, patrons, or their children. The religious or devotional poetry is early and late. Hall's psalmody was an experiment in a poetic plain style, soon given up; he wrote anthems when Bishop of Exeter, but only three were printed. None of Hall's verse is great poetry but not simply because of its kind. His métier was prose. As a poet he had an honest competence but not the genius that could make the occasional poetry of Milton or the devotional poetry of Donne distinguished. Besides, poetry for Hall was always a sideline; after 1612 he gave it up almost entirely.

Hall's poetry has its value, however. The occasional poems reflect Hall's moral and religious views during the early part of his career—indeed throughout his career, for Hall can never be said to have changed his mind philosophically. In the very conventionality of their conception, the poems suggest what a young man of Hall's temperament and education might think about a variety of subjects; they reveal Hall's characteristic, but in no way peculiar, sensitivity to the formal and metrical demands of literary genres; and the two poetic prefaces to Donne's *Anniversaries* have a real, though rarely acknowledged, significance as literary criticism. For the value of his devotional verse we must look to other standards. His "metaphrase" (as he called it) of the psalms and his anthems are polished and competent but neither profound nor moving. Hall wanted Herbert's

66

art and Donne's penchant for self-exploration and self-discovery. An essentially private man, he wrote poetry only when he could justify it in terms of his Christian morals.

I *Occasional Poems*

Hall's occasional verse consists of several funeral elegies and epitaphs, his *Kings Prophecie*, and commendatory verses or poetical prefaces to the works of Joshua Sylvester, William Bedell, and John Donne. This kind of poem (and its various subspecies) played an important role in Elizabethan and Jacobean social life since in an age before newspapers it publicized as well as celebrated events of public importance and persons of note and reinforced societal values and goals. Governed by rules of decorum and traditions of form, "occasional" poetry required stylized postures and conventional sentiments. To moderns this genre is not appealing; devoted to self-expression, we prefer the lyric cry to the mannered rhetoric of public poetry. In Hall's day, however, it was a rare poet who did not write some occasional verse and in so doing use the stock themes of its kind.

Hall wrote memorial verses on the deaths of Richard Greenham (1599), Sir Horatio Pallavicino (1600), and Prince Henry (1612). He may also have been the author of an elegy on the death of William Camden, Elizabethan schoolmaster and antiquary, who died in 1600. All these poems, not surprisingly, seem cut from the same cloth. In dignified heroic couplets, they praise the dead, console the bereaved, and do so in conventional ways.[1] The two elegies—one is more an epitaph—to Richard Greenham are epigrammatic and witty. In the first of the poems ("on the Death and Works of Master Greenham"), Hall praises Greenham, a Puritan divine he knew only by reputation, for the enduring significance of Greenham's work by creating within the compass of a dozen or so lines the image of a tree of withered yet fruitful branches whose condition symbolizes the dead author and his vital legacy. The image is unoriginal; the artifice of the poem is in the phrasing, the control of meter and rhythm—in all of which Hall is adept. In the second of the poems ("Upon his Sabboth"), Hall condenses his praise even more radically and wittily by using the topic of Greenham's best known and most influential book (*Treatise of the Sabbath*, 1599) as the basis for a reverent pun:

Whiles Greenham writeth of the Sabbath's rest,

His soul enjoys that which his pen expressed:
His work enjoyes not what it self doth say,
For it shall never find one resting day.
A thousand hands shall toss each page and line,
Which shall be scanned by a thousand eyen.
That Sabbath's rest, or this Sabbath's unrest,
Hard is to say whether is the happiest.

The ingenious elaboration of the conceit—reminiscent of the poetic strategy of Donne even in his funeral verse—seems to moderns out of keeping with the occasion. But wit on the occasion of death is too prevalent in verse of this kind to have seemed indecorous to Hall's contemporaries. Ingenuity was viewed as a good part of the poet's tribute to his subject, a way of expressing his Christian optimism and the triumph of reason over passion.

Hall wrote a short Latin elegy *(In Obitum Viri Amplissimi)* on the death of Sir Horatio Pallavicino, a sometime Papal official in England and convert to the English Church whom Hall probably knew only by reputation. He wrote a longer, and more interesting, elegy in English, consoling Lady Pallavicino, and still another epitaph ("An Epitaph") to the deceased, praising his motives for going into exile. Neither is distinguished as verse; Hall may have written the poems only because Theophilus Field, a fellow student of Hall's at Emmanuel College, had asked him to contribute something for his *An Italian's Dead Body*, the collection of memorial verses in which Hall's elegy to Lady Pallavicino was published. But the poem to Lady Pallavicino, longer and richer in thought, contains some good lines.

Hall's "Certain Verses Written and Sent in Way of Comfort to her Ladiship" aims to console the lady for her loss. His method of doing so is by refuting excessive grief as though it were an intellectual position. Hall argues, not very originally, that although grief is natural it is properly subject to reason, which declares death inevitable and universal ("We are all pilgrims to our common skies"). It is therefore futile to mourn and also impious, for Sir Henry has passed beyond the veil of tears and now enjoys heavenly bliss. Hall's logic is fleshed out with suitable images like the turtle dove, whose grief makes it a suitable emblem for the disconsolate widow and proves "natures self doth teach us to lament." But reason, with grace as its guide, causes us to observe the same birds dying of their grief. Hall assures the lady that she and her husband will meet again, even though she may now find herself on a "stranger coast." Hall's is the sort of advice he might have given to any wellborn parishioner, reasonable and polite. The beginning lines of the poems are tactful, "conceited," and replete with graceful circumlocutions typical of society poetry:

> If those salt showers that your sad eyes have shed
> Have quenched the flame your grief hath kindled,
> Madame my words shall not be spent in vain,
> To serve for wind to chase that mournful rain. (1–4)

The couplets, full of high sentence, are self-contained and epigrammatic:

> Both grief and loss do willing partners find,
> In every eye, and every feeling mind. (9–10)

Indeed, it is not hard to imagine how much Hall must have learned about prose style from fashioning such tight-knit lines of verse, where all the discipline is to put a maximum of sense in a minimum of space.

The poem "To Camden" (Davenport accepts it as Hall's)[2] consists of four eight-line stanzas of unusual rime scheme (aabcbcdd). Hall's purpose is to praise Camden as being to the writing of history what Sidney was to prose and Spenser to "numbers & heroic rhyme." Specifically, Hall praises Camden for his "Roman style" and for creating, in his histories, an "England" that can pass throughout the world beyond the seas and in the grateful memory of his country's people. The poem is full of patriotic fervor ("Long may both Englands live and living reign") and intellectually complicated in its view of Camden's histories as another "England," superior to the original in the infinity of its borders. As in his verses to Richard Greenham, Hall identifies the author with his work in order to assure the deceased that if their works survive, so shall they.

Hall's "Upon the Unseasonable Times, that Have Followed the Unseasonable Death of My Sweet Master Prince Henry," despite its somewhat ungainly title, is a short poem of twelve lines. It is the only one of Hall's funeral poems that grew out of a real relationship; yet significantly it is as impersonal as the rest. Published in the third edition of Joshua Sylvester's *Lacrymae Lacrymarum,* along with verses by Donne, Webster, Edward Herbert, and others mourning Henry's death, Hall's elegy focuses on the consequences of Henry's untimely death:

> Fond vulgar, *can'st* thou think it strange to find
> So watery winter, and so wasteful wind?
> What other face could Nature's age become,
> In looking on Great Henry's herse and tomb?
> The World's whole frame, his Part in Mourning bears,
> The winds are sighs: the rain is Heaven's tears:
> And if these tears be rife, and sighs be strong,
> Such sighs, such tears, to these sad times belong.
> These showers have drowned all hearts: these sighs did make
> The Church, the world, with griefs, with fears to shake.
> Weep on, ye Heavens; and Sigh as ye began:
> Men's sighs and tears are slight, and quickly done.

Henry died 6 November 1612; the winter that followed was characterized by storms, violent winds, and more than the usual amount of rain. In his elegy, Hall interprets these as signs of nature's mourning and supposes the fear of them universal. But although Hall's hyperbole is shocking, it is hardly unique. Prince Henry, whom Hall served as chaplain from 1608 until the Prince's death, was mourned throughout the nation and by hundreds of poets and poetasters trying to outdo each other in conceiving of what Henry's death portended. The poem offers no consolation, only a dark vision of disaster, which is really a sort of oblique praise reared on the assumption that the greater the man, the greater the effects of his death. Donne's elegy on Prince Henry operates on an identical premise.[3]

The most ambitious of Hall's occasional poems is *The Kings Prophecie, or Weeping Joy,* a conventional but interesting panegyric commemorating James' accession in 1603. It is a long poem of 384 lines with a stanza pattern (six lines, an interlocking quatrain and couplet) well suited to narrative or discursive poetry. Hall may have borrowed the idea from Spenser, who used the same stanza form in the first eclogue of his *Shepheardes Calendar,* or from Shakespeare, who put it to good service in his *Venus and Adonis.*

As his title implies, Hall's poem is both retrospective and prophetic. In the first four stanzas Hall attempts to capture the

mixed feelings of that "wondrous year" in which Elizabeth dies and
James begins his reign. Between the emotional poles of grief and
joy, Hall—and by extension the general public for whom he
speaks—reviews his dreaded anticipation of Elizabeth's death—the
fear that the great queen's passing might bring civil war, Catholic
tyranny, or Spanish invasion. Instead, royal power has passed
swiftly to the Stuart line, and most of the poem is given to a prophe
tic preview of James' accomplishments. Hall is first concerned to
depict James as a paragon of virtue and learning, a champion of true
religion. By extension, England herself comes within the purview of
Hall's panegyric; for both king and kingdom are conceived as com-
plementary entities, one lending glory to the other, God bestowing
glory on both:

> Heaven's chiefest care, Earth's second Paradise
> Wonder of Times, chief boast of Nature's style,
> Envy of Nations, president of bliss,
> Mistress of Kingdoms, Monarch of all Isles;
> World of this world, & heaven of earth, no less
> Can serve to shadow out thine happiness.
>
> Thou art the world's sole glory, he is thine;
> From him thy praise is fetched, the world's from thee,
> His from above; So the more famous been
> His rarest graces, more thy fame shall be.
> The more thy fame grows on, the fairer shoew
> His heavenly worth shall make to foreign view. (163–74)

For us, James' reign is a chapter in an old book; for Hall, it was the
beginning of a golden age in which James' "Court shall be a church
of Saints; quite free/From filth, excess and servile flattery" (293–4).
How far Hall's prophetic exuberance misled him in this expectation
is a matter of history. Certainly, however, there was nothing unique
in these expectations nor in his conception of James, whom even Sir
Francis Bacon had hailed the most learned and virtuous of kings.
Such praise of monarchs, florid and fulsome from our perspective,
was *de rigeur* in the seventeenth century. Modest praise was simply
no praise at all! Besides, Hall may have aimed his prophesy not
as a vision of what was to come but as a vision of what ought to
be, as Donne in a verse letter to the Countess of Huntingdon had

implied might be possible: ". . . oft, flatteries work as far As Counsels, and as far the endeavor raise."[4]

Despite the fact that Hall refers to the poem as "poor and plain," he evidently aimed at a grand effect. His praise of James is adorned with sweeping similes ("Like as when Tame & Ouse that while they flow . . .") and allusions to events and persons historical and mythical. Hall's rhythms are stately, the meter carefully controlled. But the grandeur often becomes pure turgidity; most modern readers will find the poem of some historical interest, but unimaginative and dull.

Commendatory verses complete the inventory of Hall's occasional verse. The little poem to William Bedell, an old school-friend of Hall's, praises Bedell's pastorals as worthy successors to those of Spenser. The poem memorializes a friendship; it cannot be taken seriously as criticism and hardly invites comment as a poem. Hall's "To Mr. Joshua Sylvester of his Bartas Metaphrases" is longer (thirty-eight lines) but equally pedestrian in conception and execution. Hall knew Sylvester too; both were in service to Prince Henry and shared a vigorous Protestantism, but Hall's appreciation had better grounds than friendship. Du Bartas' *La Semaine, ou Création du Monde* (1578—translated by Sylvester as *Divine Weeks and Works* (first collected edition, 1605)—was an immensely popular work that represented for Hall what poetry should properly do:

> I dare confess; of Muses, more than nine,
> Nor list, nor can I envy none, but thine.
> She, drenched alone in Sion's sacred Spring,
> Her Maker's praise hath sweetly chose to sing,
> And reacheth nearest the Angels notes above;
> Nor lists to sing or Tales, or Wars, or Love. (1–6)

Hall admits Sylvester's poem is only a translation, but argues that that should make no difference; "Freedom gives scope, unto the roving thought/Which by restraint is curbed." For Hall, then, Sylvester's "metaphrase" (a loose translation) imposes a beneficial aesthetic and ideological discipline. Hailing Du Bartas as "some French angel, girth with bays," Hall proclaims Sylvester the Frenchman's equal, if only the latter's translator.

Hall's skill as poet and critic is best displayed in his two prefatory poems to John Donne's *Anniversaries* on the death of Elizabeth

Drury. Hall may have met Donne as early as 1601; surely he knew Elizabeth Drury, daughter of his patrons Sir Robert and Lady Drury, from her very young girlhood.[5] When she died of a fever in 1610, Hall had as much reason as Donne to share in the Drury family's grief and to participate in Elizabeth's memorialization, even though by 1610 he no longer enjoyed the patronage of the Drurys.

Because they praise so wittily and extravagantly a young girl he knew only by reputation, Donne's *Anniversaries* have always been controversial poems. Some contemporaries thought them blasphemous; modern critics have suspected Donne's motives and developed interpretations of the long and complicated poems as ingenious as the poems themselves. Hall's prefaces are interesting as criticism because they not only execute competently the two traditional functions of the funeral elegy, praise and consolation, but also respond directly and positively to the main features of Donne's *Anniversaries*, their argument and style.

The first of Hall's poems, "To the Praise of the Dead," seeks to assuage grief for the most pathetic aspect of Elizabeth's death, its prematurity, and to praise Donne's first *Anniversarie* for its most distinctive quality, its wit. Almost after Donne's own "metaphysical" fashion, Hall's argument is a tissue of paradoxes intending to show Elizabeth's death a "gainful loss" by applying the Christian doctrines of grace and immortality to the death of a fourteen-year-old girl.

In the poem's opening lines, Hall makes the major "conceit" of Donne's first *Anniversarie*, the death of the world, serve his own purpose. Agreeing that the world is indeed dead as Donne affirms, Hall proceeds to question how this can be so, since Donne's Muse lives, forming a new world of wit:

> Well died the world, that we might live to see
> This world of wit, in his Anatomy:
> No evil wants his good: so wilder heirs
> Bedew their father's tombs with forced tears,
> Whose state requites their loss: while thus we gain,
> Well may we walk in blacks, but not complain.
> Yet how can I consent the world is dead
> While this Muse lives? which in his spirit's stead
> Seems to inform a world: and bids it be,
> In spite of loss, or frail mortality? (1–10)

Turning his attention to the "thrice noble maid," Hall argues that she could not have chosen a better time to die, since only Donne could praise her so well, and that while in life her modesty prevented her virtues from being known, in death these may be boldly praised in elegiac verses; for "Death bars reward & shame." Hall is careful to point out the divine origin of Elizabeth's virtues, building from simple theological premises (God is the source, eternal life the reward, of human virtue) to a vision of praise as communal act in which the praises sung to Elizabeth are in turn by her sung to God:

> So these high songs that to thee suited been
> Serve but to sound thy maker's praise, in thine,
> Which thy dear soul as sweetly sings to him
> Amid the choir of saints and seraphim,
> As any angel's tongue can sing of thee. (35–9)

Hall concludes his preface with the idea that given her virtues and the heavenly habitation of her soul, Elizabeth's parents grieve in vain. Her death has brought together "the cunning pencil, and the comely face," and she has taken her place amid the choir of angels. Those who survive, Donne and Hall, will keep her memory alive until they too sing her "ditty" and "note" as disembodied souls.

Although in the same style as Hall's first preface, "The Harbinger to the Progress" differs in tone and theme. Moving from the systematic analysis of the world's moribundity in Donne's first *Anniversarie* to the meditation on the state of the virtuous soul in the second, Hall's "Harbinger" represents its creator as a third party to the communion of souls Donne's "Progress of the Soul" enacts. Hall shifts from the communal "we" to the more personal "I," and his manner is less aulic, more contemplative and even affectionate. Here, Hall is not so much interested in the felicity of poet and his theme, as in praising the great spiritual powers that permit Donne to transcend so far the upper limits of mortal contemplations:

> Two souls move here, and mine (a third) must move
> Paces of admiration, and of love (1–2).

Hall's own self-disparagement dramatizes the mortal norm and defines the spiritual limitations of Donne's audience. Although Hall expresses the desire to join the movement of souls, he, and the rest of mankind, are excluded; for "no soul (whiles with the luggage of this clay/It clogged is . . .) can follow thee halfway." Meanwhile, Elizabeth's soul speeds beyond human ken, with only Donne's meditations for company:

> So fast, as none can follow thine so fast;
> Sor far as none can follow thine so far,
> (And if this flesh did not the passage bar
> Hadst caught her) let me wonder at thy flight
> Which long agone had'st lost the vulgar sight. (20–24)

In the concluding lines, Hall alludes to Donne's plan to memorialize annually Elizabeth Drury's death and endorses it, even though "more may not beseem a creature's praise":

> Still upwards mount; and let thy Maker's praise
> Honor thy Laura, and adorn thy lays.
> And since thy Muse her head in heaven shrouds
> O let her never stoop below the clouds:
> And if those glorious sainted souls may know
> Of what we do or what we sing below,
> Those acts, those songs shall still content them best
> Which praise those awful powers that make them blessed. (35–42)

Hall's own view of Donne's elegies can be contrasted with Ben Jonson's, who thought the *Anniversaries* blasphemous and pro-fane.[6] Hall, rather, supposed them meditations aimed at praising God. Donne never states his purpose so explicitly, but that Hall's interpretation is that rather than mere advice or veiled criticism of Donne's hyperbole seems likely. Hall would not so strongly have endorsed Donne's poems had he thought them impious, much less identified himself as a co-celebrant of Mistress Drury's virtues. Even more important, perhaps, is Hall's approval of Donne's wit. Hall knew Elizabeth personally, but he found nothing disrespectful in Donne's praise of her virtuous soul and nothing absurd or offen-sive about Donne's ingenious treatment of her death. Hall's prefaces are also witty, although to a lesser degree; and while they do not bare the nerves and sinews of the Metaphysical style, they are themselves ingeniously fashioned. Certainly Hall's prefaces should be considered the fullest and most informative critical response to what have often been hailed as the most important funeral poems of the century.[7]

II *Psalms*

Hall published *Some Few of David's Psalms Metaphrased* in 1607, "solicited," he explained in a preface to Samuel Burton, "by some revered friends to undertake the task, as that which seemed well to accord with the former exercises of my youth and my present profession." Despite the nonchalance this statement would seem to suggest, Hall undertook the project with definite literary principles in mind and considerable moral resolution. In an epistle to Hugh Cholmley written about the same time, Hall declared his intention to "avoid the wonted measures" which he thought "easy and least poetical" and "to keep David's entire sense, with numbers neither lofty, nor slubbered." And in his preface to Burton he observed,

The work is holy and strict, and abides not any youthful or heathenish liberty; but requires hands free from profaneness, looseness, affectation. It is a service to God and the church, by so much more carefully to be regarded as it is more common. For who is there that will not challenge a part in this labour? and that shall not find himself much more affected with holy measure rightly composed.

The preface continues as a miniature *defensio* of poetic expression, Hall pointing out to Burton, who was archdeacon of Gloucester, that since these "divine ditties" were verse in Hebrew, God could hardly be expected to object to their being so fashioned in English. But the final indication of the high seriousness with which Hall conceived of his labors is the importance of the Psalms in the religious life of the times.[8] In the seventeenth century psalm singing comprised the whole hymnody of the Anglican service. Hall's aim, therefore, was literally to put new words in the mouths of English worshipers.

He was not alone in this undertaking. The infelicities of the standard metrical version of Sternhold and Hopkins (*The Whole Book of Psalms*, 1562) was a scandal in Elizabethan England, despite its general acceptance by the pious masses, and poets as estimable as Sidney and Spenser had tried their hands at new metrical renderings with varying degrees of success. Indeed, in Hall's day metrical versions of the Psalms were a common exercise of poets, and one that had no small effect on the development of English prosody.[9]

Hall set his metaphrases to established tunes and found the sense and imagery in the language of the *Great Bible* (1539), preserved in the *Book of Common Prayer* and later to be adopted in large part in the Authorized Version of 1611. Principally Hall's concern was style. In prosody, Hall broke away from the "common measure" of Sternhold and Hopkins—the old ballad stanza with its alternating eight- and six-syllable pattern and end-stopped lines—to more varied stanza forms with run-over lines and a more natural syntax. In diction, he employed a poetic "plain style" with limited use of poetic figures and tropes and a preference for common words and expressions. The result was a poetic language suited both to its sacred themes and the understanding of the "simplest reader."

In his rendition of Psalm 6, for example, Hall found a voice for Christian penitence anticipating in its articulate plainness the devotional poetry of his co-religionist, George Herbert:

> Let me not Lord
>   be in thy wrath reproved:
> O scourge me not
>   when thy fierce rage is moved.
> Pity me, Lord,
>   that do with langour pine;
> Heal me whose bones
>   with pain dissolved been;
> Whose weary soul
>   is vexed above measure
> O Lord how long
>   shall I abide thy displeasure.

Here the standard pentameter couplet is broken into half-lines of four and six syllables. But Hall achieves more than just a redistribution of sense. Since each half line entails a brief caesural pause at its conclusion, Hall is able to keep the pace of the poem under firm control. Moreover, the metrical variety of the lines—the stressed initial syllables and feminine endings of some—gives the verse a colloquial rhythm in contrast to the monotonous regularity of meter typical of the Old Version of Sternhold and Hopkins. In the beautiful second stanza of the same psalm, Hall's phrasing, careful control of rhythm, and simple diction make his rendition much superior to the ponderous sentiments of the Prayer Book: "Turn thee, O Lord, and deliver my soul: O save me thy mercies sake. For in death no man remembreth thee: and who will give thee thanks in the pit? I am weary of groaning; every night I wash my bed: and water my couch with my tears":[10]

> Turn thee O lord
>   rescue my soul distressed;
> And save me, of thy Grace.
>   mongst those that rest,
> In silent death
>   can none remember thee;
> And in the grave
>   how shouldst thou praised be?
> Weary with sighs
>   all night I caused my bed
> To swim: with tears
>   my couch I watered.

The lines may almost be read vertically as well as horizontally; certainly the desolate condition of the petitioner is underscored by the isolation of the terse phrases of the left rank. In the final stanza of the psalm, the petitioner's despair and growing hope of redemption are reflected in lines of somber dignity:

> Deep sorrow hath
>   consum'd my dimmed eyes,
> Sunk in with grief
>   at these lewd foes of mine:
> But now hence, hence
>   vain plotters of mine ill,
> The Lord hath heard
>   my lamentations shrill;
> God heard my suit
>   And still attends the same
> Blush now, my foes,
>   And fly with sudden shame.

The plainness of Hall's psalmody may be seen in comparing it to the psalms of Sidney, a poet Hall admired but whose more opulent style he did not care to imitate. Hall's Psalm 1:3 is shaped with studied simplicity:

> He shall be like the tree,
> Set by the water springs,
> Which when his seasons be
> Most pleasant fruit forth brings:
> Whose boughs so green
> Shall never fade,
> But covered been
> With comely shade.

In contrast, Sidney's version of the same psalm is at once more expansive and more rhetorical.

> He shall be like a freshly planted tree.
>   To which sweet springs of waters neighbors be,
> Whose branches fail not timely fruit to nourish,
>   Nor withered leaf shall make it fail to flourish.
> So all the things whereto that man doth bend,
>   Shall prosper still, with well succeeding end.[11]

Hall's efforts as a psalmodist were sufficiently appreciated to require a second and third edition; but he published no more metaphrases, probably because after 1608 his clerical duties and other writing projects occupied an increasing amount of his time. Yet it is unfortunate that he did not metaphrase more of the Psalms. Certainly his do not suffer in comparison with other metrical versions of the time; and had he published more of them, Hall would probably have enjoyed a higher place among the practitioners of what in the seventeenth century was a popular poetic genre.

III *Anthems*

Hall's *Shaking of the Olive Tree*, an autobiographical memoir published in 1660, includes three anthems. These were apparently composed to be sung by choir or congregation in the cathedral of Exeter and belong to the period of Hall's bishopric there. In style, they are much like Hall's psalms, plain in diction and conventional in imagery. The first is a solemn meditation on man's fallen condition that swells in its third and fourth stanzas to a hymn in praise of God's perfection. Its theme is the contrast between man's state and God's glory as traditionally conceived in Christian theology, and the poem takes the form of a series of rhetorical questions, typified by the first stanza:

> Lord, what am I? A worm, dust, vapor, nothing!
>> What is my life? A dream, a daily dying!
> What is my flesh? My soul's uneasy clothing!
>> What is my time? A minute ever flying!
> My time, my flesh, my life, and I;
>> What are we, Lord, but vanity? (1–6)

These sobering sentiments are at least as old as Christianity itself, but there is some art in their expression. In the first line Hall effectively emphasizes man's degradation by moving, climactically, from the seemingly lowest order of being, the common worm, to yet lower orders until he reaches nonbeing. The feminine rime of lines 1–4 (Hall uses masculine rime in the final, God-centered, stanzas) conveys a sense of "falling away," a mood of dejection, suited to the stanza's tone of self-disparagement. The tetrameter couplet rounds out the stanza by echoing the four themes of the quatrain—time, flesh, life, and the person of the speaker, a structural device employed with equal success in the second stanza:

> Where am I Lord? Down in a vale of death:
>> What is my trade? Sin, my dear God offending:
> My sport, sin too; my stay, a puff of breath:
>> What end of sin? Hell's horror, never ending:
> My way, my trade, sport, stay, and place,
>> Help to make up my doleful case. (7–12)

The second anthem is a nativity hymn in crisp, tetrameter couplets, addressed to the "immortal babe," angels, shepherds, and others present at Christ's birth. The poem is joyful in tone and distinguished by its carefully controlled rhythm and apt images that convey successfully the poem's theme of paradoxical incarnation:

> Worship, ye Sages of the East,
> The King of Gods in meanness drest.
> O blessed Maid smile and adore
> The God thy womb and arms have bore. (9–12)

The third anthem, like the first, is a meditation in verse on the state of the soul, in which the speaker addresses his soul, exhorts it to leave "this baser world below," and look to heaven and "thy Savior Dear." What the soul perceives is a rather conventional conception of heaven ("Those precious gates of pearl, those streets of gold/ Those streams of life, those trees of Paradise"); but the poem, like most of Hall's poetry, is competent in prosody, even if the theme and imagery are unoriginal. In depicting heaven's glory, Hall was over his head, as who is not? The poem ends somewhat bathetically:

> See there the happy troops of purest sprites
> That live above in endless true delights;
> And see where once thyself shalt ranged be,
> And look and long for immortality;
>> And now, beforehand, help to sing
>> Hallelujahs to Heaven's King. (25–30)

Hall was not so good a poet that we regret he did not write more poems; but if he had, he might have risen in our estimation. He had a careful ear for meter and a conception of poetic diction akin to Herbert's. But after his youthful spree as a satirist and intermittent duty as an occasional poet, Hall wrote only such poetry that by the strict canons of his taste was compatible with his "graver studies." He was a moralist in his occasional poetry, conventional in his divine. His verse reminds us of some of the rarely read religious poetry of the Cavaliers, competent but a little dull, lucid but lacking the intellectual energy or profound introspection of that of the Metaphysicals. Hall's was a real, deeply felt faith. His failure to write great poetry teaches us once again how indispensable to art is *art*.

CHAPTER 5

Joseph Hall in Meditation

PERHAPS no aspect of seventeenth-century life strikes the modern reader as more remarkable than its religious passion. Milton's great themes of man's fall and redemption were central to the consciousness of his times, the last and most heroic age of faith. Nor was the passion confined to theologians and poets. Religion was the common talk of sailors and farmers, of barons and tradesmen; it was the matter of jest and motive for violence, for acts of courage and great sacrifice. The major religious upheavals of the period were popular movements; for Hall's contemporaries viewed matters of faith the way moderns view economic factors, as the determinants of political and social life. In such an atmosphere, the quest for certitude was a major cause of anxiety, as Donne had argued in his Satire III:

> On a huge hill,
> Cragged, and steep, Truth stands, and he that will \
> Reach her, about must, and about must go;
> And what the hill's suddenness resists, win so;
> Yet strive so, that before age, death's twilight,
> Thy soul rest, for none can work in that night.[1]

None can work in that night. That awesome thought must have given pause to many an Englishman in Hall's day. Convinced that the world was a stage and mortality a drama that could result in either eternal life or eternal death, Hall and his contemporaries craved sound doctrine and improving thoughts. Douglas Bush notes that more than two-fifths of the books printed in England between 1580 and 1640 were religious.[2]

The religious literature of the seventeenth century can be divided into three broad categories: collections of sermons, doctrinal

82

treatises and polemics, and manuals of practical piety and meditation. Works of the last category—guides to spiritual development through disciplined reflection on inspirational themes—proliferated during the early Stuart period and take us deep into the psychology of the age. Offering religion without vituperation, they reveal a less militant and less litigious aspect of the religious temper, an interest in personal piety and private devotion, and an anxious concern for the state of the soul. Modern scholars have done much to clarify the role meditation played in the life of the seventeenth century by indicating the popularity in England as well as on the Continent of the "exercises" of Luis de Granada, Loyola, and St. Francis de Sales; they have suggested how the mental habits acquired in meditation may have shaped the form and content of poetry.[3] But there is no doubt that meditation or "mental prayer," as St. Francis de Sales defined it, helped give the prose of the seventeenth century its introspective tone. What is Robert Burton's great *Anatomy* but an extended meditation on disease? And when Sir Thomas Browne confesses that he loves to lose himself in an "O Altitudo," he speaks not the language of science but the language of religious devotion.

Most of the devotional literature of the period is literature only in a broad, generic sense. Some of it, however, like Donne's *Devotions upon Emergent Occasions*, Lancelot Andrewes' *Private Devotions*, Jeremy Taylor's *Holy Living and Holy Dying*, and Richard Baxter's *The Saints Everlasting Rest*, are classics of their kind, illustrating both the artistry of seventeenth-century prose style and the fertile relationship of religion to literature in western culture. It is in such company that the meditations of Joseph Hall belong. His contemporary reputation was based largely on his religious writings, and it is that aspect of his work in which his devout Humanism is most fruitfully at work.

For Hall, meditation was both an habitual practice and his most sustained literary effort. From his years at Hawstead until his death in 1656, he composed literally hundreds of prose meditations expressing his religious faith and its application to moral experience. Behind Hall's endeavors was a venerable tradition of Christian meditation stretching from St. Augustine to Hugo St. Bonaventura, the corporate spiritual insights of over a thousand years of Western Christianity, and the ethical perspective of Roman Stoicism. But while Hall's motives were traditional, the literary form he gave to his thoughts was the peculiar product of his orderly imagination and the highly disciplined patterns of the Senecan manner. His meditations provide the best access to his moral philosophy and best evidence of his literary craftsmanship.

I Meditations and Vowes

Hall published two "centuries" of *Meditations and Vowes Divine and Moral* in 1605 and a third the following year.[4] As he explains in his preface to Sir Robert Drury, he made his private devotions public to fill a need for books "reducing Christianity to practice" and to secure criticism of his method. Although in light of Bush's statement there is reason to question the accuracy of Hall's belief that there was a dearth of such books, there is no reason to suspect his motives. Hall's piety was broad enough to admit humility, and his feeling that his readers were also his censors is congenial with the moderation for which he was famous. Moreover, he undoubtedly felt many handbooks to Christian life unsuited to Protestants anxious to divorce themselves from Papist ritual and superstition. In any case, that *Meditations and Vowes* went through four editions between its first publication and its collection in his *Works* (1624) suggests public reaction to Hall's devotions was generally positive.

Although Hall refers to his meditations as "homely aphorisms" his designation is somewhat misleading. Some of his meditations are indeed aphorisms, and his style is generally aphoristic; yet most of the meditations reveal systematic development through distinction, division, metaphor, proverb—traditional strategies of rhetorical development.[5] They are, like his *Epistles*, an early form of the essay; and, like Bacon's later experiments in that genre, their mode of expansion mirrors the characteristic patterns of their author's thought.[6] To Hall, however, the meditation was a distinct species of composition. Its success depended on a union of thought and feeling and that union on a definite process. In the first meditation of the first century Hall observes, "In meditation, those which begin heavenly thoughts and prosecute them not, are like those which kindle a fire under green wood and leave it so soon as it begins to flame; losing the hope of a good beginning for want of seconding it with a suitable proceeding. When I set myself to meditate, I will not give over till I come to an issue. It hath been said by some, that the beginning is as much as the midst; yea, more than all; but I say, the ending is more than the beginning" (VII, 440).

The structure of Hall's meditations reflects this concern for process. Some, consisting of single or several sentences, are like Aristotle's ethymemes, the intellectual residue of a longer but unexpressed train of thought. Most express themselves in a recurrent pattern involving the sounding of a theme—a biblical, literary, or scientific commonplace or practical observation on men and manners—the application of the theme to a religious or ethical sphere, the extraction of a principle and Hall's resolution to accommodate himself to its truth. Hall's meditations are not, from a literary point of view, uniformly successful; they vary in quality and degree of feeling and few if any are profound; but the pattern of theme, development, and resolution shows Hall's intent in meditation was not merely to express aphoristically what was often thought, but to organize ideas in such a way as to reflect the working of a mind upon which no spiritual significance is lost.

Hall's perspective in his *Meditations* is that of the Christian moralist, his matter the Christian's sojourn in a fallen world. Yet although Hall's Christianity is implicit throughout the *Meditations*, there is little in them that is expressly theological. When he turns his mind to the Church, it is not its doctrine he contemplates but its condition; and when he considers God, it is in His relationship to man and his moral consciousness. Moreover, he depends little on authority, human or sacred. Instead, Hall offers a perspective informed by the data of everyday experience—what can be known first hand through the senses or vicariously through the inherited wisdom of proverbs, and not only that data which informs the brain but that which moves the affections.

One source of such data is the operation of nature and the habits of animals. Like most of his contemporaries, Hall believed the creation a reflection of the Creator's purpose and the creatures a clue to man's moral life. The changing of the seasons, the properties of matter, and the motions of the planets, like the behavior of salamanders, elephants, pelicans, and spiders, provided not only metaphors for, but verification of, religious and ethical principles. As a consequence, the creation is for Hall both a source of wonder and instruction:

It is strange to see the varieties and proportion of spiritual and bodily diets. There be some creatures that are fatted and delighted with poisons; others live by nothing but air; and some, they say, by fire; others will taste no water, but muddy: others feed on their fellows, or perhaps on part of themselves: others,

on the execrations of nobler creatures: some search into the earth for suste-
nance, or dive into the waters; others content themselves with what the upper
earth yields them, without violence. (VII, 484)

These curious tastes, Hall continues, find counterparts in the
human soul:

Mankind, therefore hath within itself his goats, chameleons, salamanders,
camels, wolves, dogs, swine, moles, and whatever sorts of beasts: there are
but a few men amongst men. To a wise man, the shape is not so much as the
qualities. (VII, 485)

Hall's contemplation of the "Book of Creatures" leads often to a
recognition of man's moral obliquity. Unlike man, fallen from his
previously exalted station through Adam's transgression, animals
possess a consciousness of their place in the hierarchy of things.
While man remains the best of creatures, he is less happy than they,
abuses his gift of reason, and must look to animals to learn good
qualities:

It grieves me to see all other creatures so officious to their Maker in their
kind: that both winds and sea, and heaven and earth, obey him with all
readiness; that each of these hears other, and all of them their Creator; though
to the destruction of themselves: and man only is rebellious. (VII, 482)

The chief matter of Hall's meditation, however, is human behavior as observed in experience or transmitted through proverb or
commonplace, for Hall found the society of men, like nature, a
school of instruction and the elements of human commerce—trade,
agriculture, housekeeping, and hunting—metaphors of the moral
life. That Hall's reflections on such matters so often begin with
received wisdom and continue to affirm it has led to the charge of
unoriginality. But the originality of Hall's *Meditations* is not in the
novelty of their thought, but in composition that "imitates" a mind
discovering spiritual truth in ordinary experience.

In the meditation below, Hall begins with a familiar commonplace, man as microcosm, applies it to a devotional sphere, and
concludes on a note of personal resolution:

As man is a little world, so every Christian is a little church within
himself. As the Church therefore is sometimes in the wane through perse-

cution, other times in her full glory and brightness; so let me expect myself sometimes drooping under temptations, and sadly hanging down the head for the want of the feeling of God's presence, at other times carried with the full sail of a resolute assurance to heaven; knowing, that as it is a Church at the weakest stay, so shall I, in my greatest dejection, hold the child of God. (VII, 456)

The meditation comes full circle, the initial equation of man and church echoing and amplified in the conclusion and drawing Hall's thought into coherence. The language is plain but expressive, the metaphors simple. The effect for which Hall strives is not a metaphysical shudder, but a sense of order and heightened awareness of the moral suggestiveness of common images. For Hall, such an awareness is rewarded by composure—an ethical posture that can accommodate both religious exhilaration and spiritual lassitude.

Although Hall tends to confirm received truth, he rarely does so without first exploring its moral implications and applying them to his own personal situation. In Meditation 20 from the *Third Century,* Hall uses an observation of Heraclitus as impetus for reflection on dreams, as ethical behavior and as self-revelation:

It was a witty and true speech of that obscure Heraclitus, that all men, awaking, are in one common world; but when we sleep, each man goes into a several world by himself; which though it be but a world of fancies, yet is the true image of that little world which is in every man's heart; for the imaginations of our sleep show us what our disposition is, awaking: and as many in their dreams reveal those their secrets to others which they would never have done awake; so all may and do disclose to themselves in their sleep those secret inclinations, which, after much searching, they could not have found out waking. I doubt not therefore but as God heretofore, hath taught future things in dreams, which kind of revelation is now ceased, so still he teacheth the present estate of the heart this way. Some dreams are from ourselves, vain and idle, like ourselves; others are divine, which teach us good, or move us to good: and others devilish, which solicit us to evil. Such answer commonly shall I give to any temptation in the day, as I do by night. I will not lightly pass over my very dreams. They shall teach me somewhat; so neither night nor *nor* day shall be spent unprofitably: the night shall teach me what I am, the day what I should be. (VII, 494)

Although this meditation will interest moderns largely in its anticipation of Freud, it is perhaps most significant as an example of

Hall's use of "authorities." The inherited wisdom of Hall's meditation is largely proverbial; he rarely cites ancient or modern authors,
and when he does, the reference provides an impetus to thought,
not its substance. The philosophy of Heraclitus survives only in
fragments, but his oracular pronouncements were often quoted in
antiquity and in the Renaissance. It is impossible to know where
Hall came across this utterance, but it is indicative of his independence of mind that allusions to Heraclitus in Seneca are negative,
emphasizing the Greek philsopher's weakness. Here, Hall takes
Heraclitus' observation but amplifies it according to his own moral
and psychological bias. While affirming that dreams are private
worlds, he insists that they are true images of the heart, keys to
disposition and secret inclination. Classifying dreams as personal,
satanic, and divine, he posits the external forces that shape human
character and account (according to Hall's theology) for its destiny.
Finally, he incorporates dreams within the purview of his own ethical consciousness, numbering even the visions of the night among
the experiences he finds morally instructive. The Heraclitean principle is indeed affirmed, but only after its implications have been
explored, radically qualified in terms of Hall's theology, and adapted
to his personal morality.

   Although Hall's wisdom is largely proverbial, many of his meditations have a more personal provenance. His sentiments on factionalism in religion proceed from direct confrontation with Brownists, Presbyterians, and Arminians, his reflections on hypocrisy, social climbing, and ostentation from experience at university, hall,
and court. The eye of the satirist is everywhere apparent in the
sharply delineated character of the madman worldling, whose "soul
goes bare and naked, having not a rag of knowledge to cover it." And
when his theme is the state of the soul, he does not leave his own
unexamined. Although not feverishly introspective like Donne, Hall
does offer an interior perspective in his consideration of values:

   When I cast down mine eyes upon my wants, upon my sins, upon my
   miseries, methinks no man should be worse, no man so ill as I: my means so
   many, so forcible, and almost violent: my progress so small and insensible;
   my corruptions so strong; my infirmities so frequent and remediless; my
   body so unanswerable to my mind . . . (VII, 444)

And what begins a proverb may end speaking the language of the
heart's affections:

It is the basest love of all others, that is for a benefit; for herein we love not another so much as ourselves. Though there were no heaven. O Lord, I would love thee: now there is one, I will esteem it, I will desire it; yet still I will love thee for thy goodness' sake. Thyself is reward enough though thou broughtest no more. (VII, 450)

Indeed, Hall's most successful meditations fuse tradition and experience, thought and feeling.

We pity the folly of the lark, which, while it playeth with the feather and stoopeth to the glass, is caught in the fowler's net, and yet cannot see ourselves alike made fools by Satan, who, deluding us by the vain feathers and glasses of the world, suddenly enwrappeth us in his snares. We see not the nets, indeed: it is too much that we shall feel them, and that they are not so easily escaped after as before avoided. *O Lord, keep thou mine eyes from beholding vanity.* And though mine eyes see it, let not my heart stoop to it, but loathe it afar off. And if I stoop at any time and be taken, set thou my soul at liberty that I may say, *My soul is escaped, even as a bird out of the snare of the fowler: the snare is broken, and I am delivered.* (VII, 466)

In a characteristic maneuver, Hall transforms a simple image to symbol, and the spectacle of the lark's capture is changed to the more significant drama of man's tragic stooping to delusion. As in his best meditations, Hall achieves an eloquent compromise between Senecan rigidity and the idiom and rhythm of colloquy. The Psalmist's exalted cry of delivery is woven deftly into the texture of Hall's own rhetoric, giving the experience of the meditation a quality of universality and the meditation itself unity and expressiveness.

II *The Art of Meditation*

Encouraged by the success of his *Centuries* and even more convinced of the public's interest in practical piety, Hall published in 1606 his *Art of Divine Meditation.* This work, unlike the *Centuries,* is pedagogical. Hall's purpose is to advance meditation as a beneficial practice incumbent upon all Christians, to outline procedures, and to exemplify them in a short prose meditation on "death" that serves as appendix to the treatise. Thus, if Hall's *Centuries* reduce Christianity to practice, his *Art of Meditation* abstracts his practice through theory.

In his *Art,* Hall defined meditation as "a bending of the mind upon some spiritual object through diverse forms of discourse, until our thoughts come to an issue" and distinguished two kinds of meditation: the "extemporal" or that which fixes on the "book of creatures" and the "deliberate" or that "wrought out of our own heart." Both types, according to Hall, move the affections toward godliness; and here, as in several meditations of the *Centuries*, Hall insists on the importance of emotion in religious experience, for meditation can not come to an issue until its truth is apprehended by the emotions as well as the intellect.

For the first kind of meditation, the extemporal, Hall provides no rule. Since its subject matter is infinite, its practice cannot be prescribed; so Hall devotes only a few pages in its discussion. Yet its practice is no less obligatory to the Christian. Hall observes that such meditation is ancient (he cites Solomon, the Psalmist, Jesus, and Augustine as practitioners) and the means by which the believers gain access to "the thought and discourse of that excellent order which God hath settled in all these inferior things." Indeed he insists that if the spiritual significance of the creatures be overlooked, the creation itself is "half lost": "God is wronged, if his creatures be unregarded; ourselves most of all, if we read this great volume of the creatures, and take out no lesson for our instruction" (VI, 49).

Hall undoubtedly would have classed most of the meditations in his *Centuries* as extemporal, and thus many of the procedures discussed in the *Art* are only partially relevant to Hall's actual practice. Yet it must be remembered that Hall's purpose was not to have Christians write essays, but to encourage them to meditate. His discussion of deliberate meditation, then, aims to accommodate an audience of average persons who will bend their minds in private devotion, not necessarily in literary expression.

Hall expounds his *Art* with characteristic clarity and orderliness. He is first concerned to explain the conditions under which meditation is possible. A person fit for meditation must be sincere in intent, be free from worldly thoughts, and be constant; for meditation is habitual; it cannot be successfully practiced unless regularly scheduled. Further it can be practiced only in solitude. Hall is willing to leave to his reader's discretion the fittest place for contemplation, observing that Jesus meditated on the mount, John the Baptist in the wilderness, and Chrysostom in his bath. "It matters not, so he be solitary and silent." The time of meditation is similarly at the discretion of the reader, although Hall notes that he prefers the evening and walking to other times of day and postures.

The chief business of Hall's *Art* is the order of deliberate meditation, which must follow certain steps if what begins in the brain is to end in the heart. Essentially, Hall's program consists of three parts: an introductory prayer, the "deep and firm consideration of the thing propounded," and a sequence of complaints, petitions, and commendations in which the matter of meditation is interiorized and the affections moved. For the reader's convenience, Hall provides a diagram showing the various steps of contemplation and suggesting the increasing rigor of thought necessary to bring the meditation to "issue." The source of this program, Hall admits, is the work of an obscure and nameless monk, written over a century before.[7] But Hall in fact owes more to his Cambridge education than to an anonymous monk, for although Hall consoles the unlearned reader with the assurance that "deep and firm consideration" follows the course of "natural reason" and that "we are all thus far born logicians," Hall's method of exploration follows essentially the heuristic scheme of Ramist logic.

In that scheme, content for discourse was generated by a systematic investigation of the subject at hand. Accordingly, Hall advises his reader first to begin meditation with a description of the chosen topic, next to divide the topic into its parts or aspects, then to contemplate its cause and effect with its attendant circumstances, and to conceptualize further the matter of meditation by comparison and contrast. Finally, Hall's reader is encouraged to resort to the "pregnant testimonies of scripture." Hall allows the possibility that such a method is not suitable for every meditator: "I desire not to bind every man to the same uniform proceeding in this part. Practice and custom may perhaps have taught other courses, more familiar, and not less direct." He also explains that the practitioner need not feel obligated to exhaust all these "logical places" and warns him against striving more for logic than devotion. But he is confident that his method will excite feeling as well as generate content; and for the reader perplexed by the difficulties of his procedure, he provides a model meditation on death, following his own rules, at the conclusion of the treatise.

Reformation fervor notwithstanding, devout Protestants often found directions for meditation in Catholic handbooks;[8] yet Hall's

Art is thoroughly Protestant. Hall alludes to Origen, Augustine, Bernard, Gerson, but he does so largely to advance the superiority of his own method. He scrupulously avoids reference to the most influential Catholic practitioners of his day, Fray Luis de Granada and, most importantly, St. Ignatius Loyola, even though he surely knew their works. Indeed, Hall owes little or nothing to the Catholics in his *Art*. He shares Loyola's view that "it is not the abundance of knowledge that fills and satisfies the soul but to feel and relish things interiorly;[9] and Hall follows Gerson in allowing his readers to use whatever system they feel is most comfortable. But Hall's agreement on these principles hardly argues indebtedness. The distinguishing marks of the Ignatian method—the strict regimen, systematic self-examination, and "composition of place" and "colloquy"—are conspicuously absent from Hall's program; and unlike Gerson, Hall is interested in heightened moral awareness and spiritual fitness, not mystical realization. Moreover, as Frank L. Huntley has suggested, Hall's extemporal contemplation of the book of creatures harkens back to an older meditational system not featured in the Catholic treatises most influential in Hall's day.[10] And in his discussion of themes suitable for deliberate meditation Hall not only excludes some subject matter traditional to Catholic piety—e.g. the Blessed Virgin, the Seven Sacraments—but also includes Protestant topics like "the certainty of our election" and "the proceeding of our sanctification." Finally, Hall's use of Ramist invention as a means of exploring meditational themes further shows his Protestant bias. Ramus had died a victim of the St. Bartholomew's Day Massacre in 1572 and subsequently had been acclaimed a Protestant martyr. His revision of the classical discipline of rhetoric and logic had been widely accepted in Protestant circles and especially at Cambridge, which had become at some of its colleges during the last decades of the sixteenth century as much a Ramist as a Protestant stronghold. The *Art* then, while only of partial relevance to Hall's literary meditations, is an index to his religious and intellectual orientation.

It is also an index to his style, for Hall's directions in the *Art* assume the characteristic shape of his discourse. Building on the premise that his program is reasonable, he finds his rules in proverb and adage. In advocating prayer at the beginning of meditation, he observes that "a goodly building must show some magnificence in the gate; and great personages have seemly ushers to go before them, who by their uncovered heads command reverence and way." And shortly thereafter, his description of the orderly process of meditational fashion breaks into isocolonic periods: "It [meditation] begins in the understanding, endeth in the affection; it begins in the brain, descends to the heart; begins on earth, ascends to heaven; not suddenly, but by certain stairs and degrees, till we come to the highest."

III Contemplations Upon the . . . Holy Story

To Hall, God revealed himself in two ways—through His Works and through His Word—and Hall's most ambitious literary undertaking was, as its title suggests, a prolonged literary meditation on central scenes from the Old and New Testaments: *Contemplations upon the Principal Passages of Holy Story*, published in eight volumes over a period of more than twenty years (1612–1634).

Despite the magnitude of Hall's undertaking, His *Contemplations* was a labor of love. In one of his many dedicatory prefaces he describes its composition as a "divine task, wherein I cannot but profess to place so much contentment as that I wish not any other measure of my life than it." In another, he views his work as a refuge from the vituperation of religious controversy. In still another, he sees it as recreative. But his sustaining conviction was that the *Contemplations* was edifying, not as paraphrase or gloss but as a presentation of scripture emotionally as well as intellectually apprehended; for although Hall often accused his age of wanting doctrine, his greatest censure was that it lacked feeling.

Hall furnished his *Contemplations* with many dedicatory prefaces to prominent persons of his day. These provide useful insights into his attitudes toward history, both sacred and profane. In general, Hall shares the premises of his age: human history is a book of rule and example. From it, one learns of man's nature, for his nature is constant; and in it, one finds paradigms of virtue and vice, wisdom and folly. It is, as is all creation for Hall, a source of instruction as well as delight. Sacred history, on the other hand, is superior to the profane. Its matter is not only more ancient but more varied and magnificent; and unlike secular history, it teaches not only what *is* but what *should be*. Most significantly, it is God's own history: an emanation of His will and a prophesy of things to come. Hall also thinks of the scriptures as a *speculum principis*, a "mirror" for princes. In his dedicatory preface to the first volume of the *Contem-*

plations he tells Prince Henry, "Here your highness shall see how the great pattern of princes, the King of Heaven, hath ever ruled the world; how his substitutes, earthly kings, have ruled it under him, and with what success either of glory or ruin. Both your peace and war shall find here holy and great examples." Hall's *Contemplations* is thus a counterpart to his *Meditations and Vowes.* In one Hall opened the Book of Creatures, in the other the Book of Scripture. In both he found the sort of spiritual nourishment he delighted in making public.

The distinguishing characteristics of the *Contemplations* are the simplicity of its style, its dramatic presentation of narrative materials, and the conspicuous absence of the normal paraphernalia of seventeenth-century exegesis: learned allusions, Latin and Greek quotations, dogma and polemics, or textual criticism. Instead, Hall speaks plainly and without resort to "sources" other than the sacred text itself. Kinlock has suggested that Hall conceived of his work as a new mode of biblical interpretation.[11] But although Hall's approach is neither allegorical or analytical (the prevailing modes of his day), he in fact does not seem interested in exegesis at all. When Hall wished to explicate, he paraphrased, as in his *Paraphrase upon the Hard Texts of the Whole Divine Scripture* (1633), a compendious summary written for the "plain reader." In his *Contemplations,* on the other hand, Hall strove not merely to paraphrase passages but to apprehend their content visually and interiorly.

Like his *Meditations and Vowes,* Hall's *Contemplations* follows a method. Working chronologically through the Old and New Testaments, Hall selects passages of dramatic incident, developing each into a "composition" of three to five pages, embroidered with detail, character analysis, and moral reflection. Of chief importance to Hall is that each scene be visualized. Each of his many dedicatory prefaces features a preview to the action of that book. The reader is told what he will see and sometimes what he will hear; and Hall fulfills this promise by referring to his vignettes as "seen," "heard," or "felt"; by shifting into the present tense; and by breaking the narrative into segments, so that each element in a sequence can be perceived as a discrete and significant action. Further, Hall speculates on the appearance, motives, character, history, and future of biblical figures, often providing them with dimensions only implied in the sacred text. And, finally, Hall refuses to move from one aspect of action to the next before the scene has been emptied of its thematic content. Believing the Bible inspired, he finds no event without its moral or prophetic significance. The following description of Abraham journeying with his son Isaac to the child's sacrifice is typical as a mixture of narrative, character analysis, and moral summary:

> The good patriarch rises early, and addresses himself to his sad journey. And now must he travel three whole days to this execution; and still must Isaac be in his eye, whom all this while he seems to see bleeding upon the pile of wood which he carries: there is nothing so miserable as to dwell under the expectation of a great evil; that misery which must be is mitigated with speed, and aggravated with delay. All this while, if Abraham had repented him, he had leisure to return. (I, 36)

Later in the same episode, Hall amplifies the biblical account, probing the terrors of both father and son, heightening the irony and pathos of Abraham's predicament, and developing the laconic patriarch of Genesis into a more copious spokesman for his own reluctant execution of God's command:

> The heavy tidings were loath to come forth; it was a death to Abraham to say what he must do: he knows his own faith to act this, he knows not Isaac's to endure it. But now when Isaac hath helped to build the altar whereon he must be consumed, he hears, not without astonishment, the strange command of God, the final will of his father. "My son, thou art the lamb which God hath provided for this burnt offering: if my blood would have excused thee, how many thousand times had I rather to give thee mine own life than take thine! Alas! I am full of days, and now, of long, lived not but in thee: thou mightest have preserved the life of thy father, and have comforted his death, but the God of us both hath chosen thee: he that gave thee unto me miraculously, bids me by an unusual means return thee unto him. I need not tell thee that I sacrifice all my worldly joys, yea, and myself, in thee; but God must be obeyed; neither art thou too dear for him that calls thee: come on, my son, restore that life that God hath given thee by me: offer thyself willingly to these flames; send up thy soul cheerfully unto thy glory; and know that God loves thee above others, since he requires thee alone to be consecrated in sacrifice to himself. (I, 36–7)

In each of Hall's *Contemplations* Hall's interest in the conflicting passions from which moral decisions must come is always evident. Indeed, his tendency is to "load" the scenes with a degree of emotional ferment that often ends in melodrama:

Who cannot imagine with what perplexed mixtures of passions, with what changes of countenance, what doubts, what fears, what amazement, good Isaac received this sudden message from the mouth of his father, how he questioned, how he pleaded? But when he had somewhat digested his thoughts, and considered that the author was God, the actor Abraham, the action a sacrifice, he now approves himself the son of Abraham; now he encourages the trembling hand of his father with whom he strives in this praise of forwardness and obedience; now he offers his hands and his feet to the cords, his throat to the knife, his body to the altar; and growing ambitious of the sword and fire, intreats his father to do that which he would have done though he had dissuaded him. (I, 37)

Although Hall's perspective is omniscient, the *Contemplations* is designed to imply his own intimate relationship to the events he reenacts, and his personal biases are everywhere apparent. They must be so, if his audience is to find in Hall's own response to the sacred vignettes a model for their own. One kind of expression found in the *Contemplations* is the exclamation of approval or disapproval. Thus, Hall responds to his own account of Isaac's acquiescence with verbal cheers ("O holy emulation of faith! O blessed agreement of the sacrificer"); and when he moralizes on the significance of the entire episode, Hall makes of that meaning a personal as well as universal axiom: "Whatsoever is dearest to us upon earth is our Isaac; happy are we if we can sacrifice it to God: those shall never rest with Abraham that cannot sacrifice with Abraham."

Twentieth-century readers, accustomed to the objectivity and swift pace of modern fiction, are likely to find Hall's narrative slow and gratuitously glossed. But Hall, although using fictional techniques such as invented speeches and character analysis to dramatize his matter, has little interest in the story for its own sake. Whether Hall's subject is Adam's fall or Christ's crucifixion, the scene is envisioned to make it immediate, and made immediate so that its meaning might be taken to the heart. His treatment of the Sacrifice of Isaac is a case in point. One of the best known of Old Testament episodes, Abraham's subjection to God's command was historically interpreted as a prefiguration of God's sacrifice of Christ. It was not something that happened, but something caused to happen so an even greater event might be foreshadowed. Hall's moralizing thus builds on the innate didacticism of the episode and indeed, upon the didacticism of sacred history in general. All scrip-

ture is given for our instruction, St. Paul had affirmed: characteristically, Hall dwells on the scene not as type but as a moral exemplum.
We learn from the obedience of Abraham and Isaac about the
exigencies of obedience, just as we learn (among other things) to be
valiant and modest from Samson, to be merciful from Zacchaeus,
and to forego envy, scrupulousness, ignorance, and pride from the
example of the discontented Jews. "It is edification we affect, and
not curiosity" (II, 511).

It is not difficult to account for the popularity of the *Contemplations* in Hall's own time or in the century that followed. To generations committed to Bible reading, Hall's *Contemplations* not only
brought alive the mythical figures of scripture, but dramatized their
actions and analyzed their emotions. The popularity of the *Contemplations* depended as well on their exposition of the familiar and the
true—the moral commonplaces and received ideas that made God's
sacred book, like His "Book of Creatures," a handbook of ethics and
a practical psychology. The perfidy of Saul and the virtue of
Jonathan, the goodness of Eli and the wickedness of his son, determined for Hall an issue over which post-Freudian psychologists still
wrangle: "If the conveyance of grace were natural, holy parents
would not be so ill-suited with children" and vice versa. In his
preface to the fifth volume of his *Contemplations* he advises Lord
Russel of Thornbaugh that from Shemaiah's curses, Arithophel's
fortunes, and the blood of Absalom and Sheba, he may learn, respectively, of the vulnerability of the great and innocent to mali-
cious tongues, how "witless and insensate craft is when it strives
against honesty," and the terrible consequences of rebellion.
Throughout the *Contemplations* it is evident that Hall views sacred
history the way he views the creation, as a mine of moral, political,
and theological instruction.

The *Contemplations* was one of Hall's most sustained efforts. In it
he tried to make familiar Bible stories clear, vivid, and morally
pertinent. His purpose, as we have seen, was not merely to paraphrase, but analyze character and motive, to extract lessons for
life, to move the mind and heart of the reader to a greater faith in
Divine Providence. For Hall, the *Contemplations* was also an exercise in composition. In a preface to volume 9, he explains that his
habit was to treat scriptural matter first in sermons, then to gather
the "quintessence of those larger discourses into these forms of
meditation." Thus, while he preached the word he practiced the

writer's craft, honing his pen in the elusive art of making old stories new, hard meanings plain. It is indicative of the high value he placed on the *Contemplations* that it, rather than the sermons, was the "quintessence" of his thought. Moderns may prefer their scripture unglossed and unadorned. But to Hall, elaboration on the original was a sincere form of devotion, and much needed if the sacred stories were to be feelingly apprehended.

IV   Occasional Meditations

Hall's last important series of devotional exercises was his *Occasional Meditations* (1630). Composed during his years as Bishop of Exeter, this collection of 140 essays (forty-nine were added to the original ninety-one in the edition of 1633) was published by his son to demonstrate "how holy minds have been ever wont to look through these bodily objects at spiritual and heavenly." Like other devotional works by Hall, the *Occasional Meditations* proved popular, and Hall himself thought highly enough of it to provide a Latin translation in 1635.

The meditations of this group follow the pattern of Hall's *Meditations and Vowes.* The short essays tend to fall into a tripartite division of theme, application, and resolution or prayer; and the mode of intellection is the one habitual to Hall: a recognition of correspondences and analogies and the formulation of moral axioms. The distinctive feature of this series, however, is that Hall's thought is activated by sights, smells, and sounds, rather than proverbs and commonplaces. As a consequence, the *Occasional Meditations* is both more descriptive and more personal than his earlier devotions and his style is less sententious. The data of experience—the sight of sundials, open graves, children playing, ruins decaying, smells of flowers, medicines, and the pealing of bells and songs of birds—are treated as "glasses" through which the spiritual eye perceives a multitude of eternal truths.

The third essay of the series, "Upon the sight of an eclipse of the sun," is typical:

Light is an ordinary and familiar blessing; yet so dear to us, that one hour's interception of it sets all the world in wonder. The two great luminaries of heaven, as they impart light to us, so they withdraw light from each other: the sun darkens the full moon, in casting the shadow of the earth upon her opposed face: the new moon repays this blemish to the sun, in the interposing of her dark body betwixt our eyes and his glorious beams: the earth is troubled at both.

O God, if we be so afflicted with the obscuring of some piece of one of thy created lights for an hour or two, what a confusion shall it be, that thou, who art the God of these lights, in comparison of whom they are mere darkness, shalt hide thy face from thy creature for ever! O thou, that art the Sun of Righteousness, if every of my sins cloud thy face, yet let not my grievous sins eclipse thy light. Thou shinest always, though I do not see thee; but, O, never suffer my sins so to darken thy visage that I cannot see thee. (X, 122)

The range of Hall's interests in these meditations is broad. Some of his subjects—an open grave, the starry heavens, or flowers in the field—are traditional meditative themes. But Hall also meditates at the sight of flies swarming to a horse's wound, upon feeling numbness in his arm, and upon witnessing a harlot carted through a clamorous crowd. He finds food for thought in blind men, fools, dwarfs, left-handed men, and a blackamore in the road, and in the quenching of a hot iron in water, the drying of herbs, and the shutting of one eye. The effect of such variety is that the *Occasional Meditations* gives an impression of Hall moving around in his world, of strolling in his garden, walking down country roads or through city streets. We also get some idea of the world itself, in its largest and most miniscule features. The sight of a ruined cottage is captured in a few stark details: moldered and clay walls; a thin, uncovered roof; bending studs; dark and broken windows. The thrill of childhood games is imaginatively relived: "Now that there is a handful of cherry-stones at the stake, how near is that boy's heart to his mouth for fear of his playfellow's next cast, and how exalted with desire and hope of his own speed" (X, 140). Hall vividly depicts the public abasement of the harlot: "The streets are not more full of beholders than clamours. Every one strives to express his detestation of the fact by some token of revenge: one casts mire, another water, another rotten eggs, upon the miserable offender" (X, 165). Hall also observes the habits of bees, spiders, wasps, and worms.

But Hall is a moralist, not a scientist; while his interests are broad, he is careful to define their emphasis. He delights in the beauties of the world, responds to nature, to music, to broad vistas and displays of color and sound. He calls smell the "meanest and least useful of the senses" but declares that there is no other that gives "so exquisite contentment" and finds that "there is no earthly thing that yields so perfect a pleasure to any sense as the odour of the first rose doth to the scent" (X, 166). Elsewhere, he admires the stars, those "goodly spangles of light above our heads" (X, 168). Man's works are equally wondrous to him. Upon hearing a well-played lute he exclaims, "Had we lived in some rude and remote part of the world, and should have been told that it is possible, only by an hollow piece of wood, and the guts of beasts stirred by the fingers of men, to make so sweet and melodious a noise, we should have thought it utterly incredible" (X, 160). But Hall, while sensitive, is also suspicious of sensation. His salvation at stake, he must see things as they are; for evaluation depends on perception, and evaluation is a moral act. As a gold coin on the bottom of a stream seems twice its size because of the medium through which it is perceived, so objects may be misconceived and wrongly evaluated through the medium of the perceiver. The condition of the soul is therefore important, for the carnal mind is doomed to deception. "If we look with carnal eyes through the interposed mean of sensuality, every base and worthless pleasure will seem a large contentment; if with weak eyes we shall look at small and immaterial truths aloof off, in another element of apprehension, every parcel thereof shall seem main and essential" (X, 147).

That perception is dependent on morality is fundamental to Hall's meditative practice. In "Upon a pair of spectacles" Hall makes his doctrine explicit. His spectacles are not sight but aids to sight. Hall's philosophy is dualistic but not Platonic. Bodily objects are not emanations of the divine; they have, rather, a real but finite existence and one, therefore, of infinitely less worth than spiritual objects. Rightly perceived, they are not ends in themselves, but means to knowledge of what lies beyond the veil. Following the precept of St. Paul, Hall sees mortality as a glass through which we see darkly, although with varying degrees of clarity depending on our spiritual condition. To the carnal mind, a bee is just a bee; to the spiritual, a bee is a lesson in social ethics. The material world, then, is not a reflection but an emblem of things beyond.

Yet, although Hall emphasizes the primacy of faith over reason, he does not discount reason or disparage human learning in favor of revelation. Sense perception plays its part in the drawing of analogies, a rational faculty. Spiritual insights of the kind demonstrated by Hall are furthermore limited to rational beings. Like a true Humanist, Hall loves books; and although he proclaims with Solomon that there is no end of making them, he both endorses the advancement of learning and the divine gifts which make it possible: "God hath given to man a busy soul, the agitation whereof cannot but through time and experience work out many hidden truths; to suppress these, would be no other than injurious to mankind, whose minds, like unto so many candles, should be kindled by each other" (X, 154). Furthermore, Hall surely felt his *Occasional Meditations* a contribution to that illumination, if not for the matter, then for the example. As he notes in the Proem, "Our active soul can no more forbear to think, then the eye can choose but see when it is open. To do well, no object should pass us without use. Everything that we see reads us new lectures of wisdom and piety."

The style of *Occasional Meditations* may be described as a relaxation of Hall's earlier manner. Sentences are more varied in length, looser in construction, and more flexible in rhythm. Hall remains fond of aphorisms, but the trenchant phrase is less conspicuous. To achieve an imitation of the mind awed by what it observes and committed to extracting from the observation all that it may, Hall makes his language more effusive, more poetic: "All harmonious sounds are advanced by a silent darkness"(X, 142). And to suggest an intimacy with his audience he adopts a tone of quiet deliberation, rendering the meditation a shared experience:

I know not what horror we find ourselves at the sight of a serpent. Other creatures are more loathsome, and some no less deadly than it; yet there is none at which our blood riseth so much as at this. Whence should this be, but out of an instinct of our old enmity? We were stung in paradise, and cannot but feel it. But here is our weakness; it was not the body of the serpent that could have hurt us without the suggestion of sin; and yet we love the sin while we hate the serpent. (X, 156)

Hall teaches by inviting his reader to explore with him the paradoxes of his theme, and to discover the truth behind all sense experience.

V *Shorter Collections*

Not surprisingly, given the straightened circumstances of Hall's last years, most of his writings during that period are meditative. Chief among these are *Breathings of the Devout Soul* (1648), *Susurrium Cum Deo* (1650), and *The Invisible World Discovered to Spiritual Eyes* (1651). Hall's *Breathings* consists of forty-nine prose meditations, each a paragraph in length, focusing on the relationship of the soul to its maker. Hall apparently conceived of the meditations as the soul's soliloquies, and there is a distinctively Augustinian tone of self-effacement in the presence of God's omnipotence, mercy, and mystery. A tripartite organizational scheme recalls the general plan of Hall's earlier meditations: first there is a statement or query, then some discussion—usually an elaboration of the query or statement with example, and finally an application of the spiritual principle to himself and an appeal for divine aid. Hall's prose is characteristically aphoristic but somewhat less so than in his *Meditations and Vowes*, perhaps because here he wished to stress the deeply personal provenance of this thought. And, indeed, in various of the meditations, he manages a truly personal note:

Lord God, what a wearisome circle do I walk in here below. I sleep, and dress, and work, and eat, and work again, and eat again, and undress, and sleep again; and thus wearing out my time, find satiety in all these, troublesome. Lord, when shall I come to that state wherein I shall do nothing but enjoy thee, do nothing but praise thee; and in that one work I shall find such infinite contentment, that my glorified soul cannot wish to do any other; and shall therein alone bestow a blessed eternity? (VIII, 10)

Despite the implication of its subtitle ("Soliloquies or Holy Self-Conferences of the Devout Soul") that *Susurrium Cum Deo* is a sequel to Hall's *Breathings*, the eighty-odd meditations in this collection are longer, broader in scope, and looser in structure. Each piece in the series is titled and concludes with Hall's customary application of spiritual or moral truth to himself and an appeal. Almost all of the themes in the series Hall treated earlier in his career in either his moral or meditative writings, but here in the prose style of his last years Hall found a more natural and relaxed idiom in which to express his thought:

We are all naturally desirous to live; and though we prize life above all earthly things, yet we are ashamed to profess that we desire it for its own sake, but pretend some other subordinate reason to affect it. One would live, to finish his building or to clear his purchase; another, to breed up his children, and to see them well matched: one would fain outlive his trial at law; another wishes to outwear an emulous corrival; One would fain out last a lease that holds him off from his long-expected possessions; another would live to see the times amend, and a reestablishment of a public peace. Thus we, that would be glad to give skin for skin, and all things for life, would seem to wish life for any thing but itself. After all this hypocrisy, nature, above all things, would live, and makes life the main end of living: but grace has higher thoughts; and therefore, though it holds life sweet and desirable, yet entertains the love of it upon more excellent, that is, spiritual terms. O God, I have no reason to be weary of this life, which, through thy mercy, long acquaintance hath endeared to me, though sauced with some bitter disgusts of age; but how unworthy shall I approve myself of so great a blessing, if now I do not more desire to continue it for thy sake than my own. (VIII, 40)

This meditation bears the title "Love of Life"; it is almost a little essay, but not quite. The orderly, logical development of Hall's themes presents a highly condensed dialectic of assertion and qualification, moving always from one level of understanding to a higher. We are reminded again that for Hall meditation was not random thought but a highly disciplined procedure that both began and ended in wisdom; for there is nothing tentative or adventitious about that procedure, and this is chiefly what distinguishes the prose meditations Hall composed from the closely-allied essay form. Nature has its reasons, Hall asserts; so must Grace; Grace must ultimately triumph over nature, just as hypocrisy ultimately gives way to truth. Hall does not feel his way to that understanding but presupposes it from the beginning in the very plan of a meditation designed to expound a principle rather than to dramatize its discovery.

The *Invisible World*, Hall's last collection, is colored by a sense of approaching death, at least as far as its subjectmatter is concerned. "I have desired," he explains in his preface, "to acquaint myself with that invisible world to which I am going; to inter-know my good God, and his blessed angels and saints." Hall thought of the work as a kind of travelogue through the unseen world of spirits, angels, and devils and set about to give an account of the nature and property of each supernatural kind. Although loosely structured, the pieces qualify as meditations since Hall always concludes by making some personal application of his doctrine to himself, but the meditations also have some of the characteristics of his polemical treatises: biblical and historical allusions and anecdotes and, occasionally, an argumentative edge. He defends the idea of guardian angels, quarrels with Catholic writers too curious in their description of angelic hierarchies. Moderns will find his view of witches quaint but thoroughly typical of his times. A passage from the second book ("Of God and his Angels") will give a taste of the whole:

> I cannot quite mislike the conceit of Reuchlin and his Cabala, seconded by Galatinus, that as in an egg the yolk lies in the midst encompassed round with the white, and that again by a film and shell; so the sensible world is inclosed within the intelligible; but, withal I must add, that here is not a mere involution only, but a spiritual permeation and inexistence; yet without all confusion. For those pure and simple natures are not capable of mingling with gross, material substances; and the God of order hath given them their own separate essences, offices, operations; as for the managing of their own spiritual commonwealth within themselves, so for the disposing, governing, and moving of this sensible world. (VIII, 147)

Like Hall's other literary endeavors, the meditations set a pattern for his generation, demonstrating both the directions Protestant meditation might profitably take and establishing a standard in style and thought. Yet Hall's influence is difficult to determine exactly. His greatest impact was undoubtedly on that audience he had sought, simple Christians seeking inspiration and moral guidance. But his meditations also proved literary models. The devotional writings of Richard Brathwaite, George Berkeley, and Arthur Warwick recall Hall's themes and procedures, while Thomas Traherne's *Centuries* echoes Hall's method of dividing his meditations into "hundreds" in *Meditations and Vowes*. Richard Baxter paid tribute to Hall's treatise in his *Saint's Everlasting Rest*, and Francis Quarles' *Divine Fancies* owes more than a little to Hall's *Occasional Meditations*.[12] Finally, Hall's preeminence is attested by his contemporaries. In a sermon preached at the Bishop's death, John Whitefoot praised him as "one of the first that taught this church the art of divine meditation"[13]; and Robert Boyle, founder of the Royal Society, in his "Discourse touching Occasional Meditations" (1665) felt constrained to justify his departure from Hall's example: "I know it is a new thing, that I have ventured to put some occasional reflections into dialogues. But the reader will be less startled at my deviating in this, and other things from Bishop Hall's way of writing occasional meditations, if I acknowledge, that not to prepossess or bias my fancy, I purposely (til of late) forbad myself the perusing of that eloquent prelate's devout reflections."[14]

For moderns, Hall's devotional works are guides to seventeenth-century attitudes. Unbookishly and unpretentiously, his reflections on man, nature, and scripture testify both to the reality of his own religious experience and to the breadth of the religious consciousness of his times. For when Hall speaks of his own proclivity for ferreting out from the data of experience inherent and eternal truths he is not only speaking for himself but for an age of writers and thinkers for whom God's will was immanent in the visible world and the discovery of that will a moral imperative. Browne mulling over old urns and Burton pondering melancholy are only variants of Hall's meditative practice. It was Hall's achievement that he passed to his successors in his century one of the literary forms in which meditation could be enacted.

A last word must be said about Hall's meditations as literature. Hall can be sententious and tediously so; his Senecan rhetoric can grate like machinery; he can also write with engaging clarity and point, and sometimes with poetic vigor and vision even though his is not the poetry of a Browne or a Donne. Certainly the aphoristic quality of his meditations has been overstressed. At its best, Hall's prose style is a flexible medium that may describe movement, express feeling, reflect the texture of experience as well as give terse expression to commonplaces. If Hall's prose does not always show such flexibility it is enough to say that it sometimes does. One must agree with Thomas Fuller that Hall is "best" in his meditations. Perhaps more than any other of his works, they support Hall's right to be remembered and read.

CHAPTER 6

Pulpit Eloquence

JOSEPH HALL was a great preacher in what has often been called
the golden age of English pulpit oratory. In his autobiography, he
tells us that he preached thrice weekly at Hawstead and Waltham;[1] he could hardly have been less busy when good fortune and
demonstrated ability saw him to royal appointments and episcopal
dignities. Of the many hundreds, perhaps thousands, of sermons
Hall must have preached during his long ministry, only forty-three
survive; but these give ample evidence of his power as a preacher.

In the seventeenth century the sermon was an important literary
form, shaping social and political attitudes, reflecting literary fashions, and demanding the full intellectual resources of a learned
clergy. Talented clerics such as Lancelot Andrewes, John Donne,
and Jeremy Taylor drew huge crowds, who sometimes listened for
more than an hour while these golden-tongued orators drew out a
line of thought, pondered a Latin etymology, or dissected a scriptural text with a meticulousness moderns would probably feel more
suited to a doctoral dissertation than a homily. The better sermons
were published, as the extensive bibliographies of sermon literature
by Herr and Mitchell suggest[2] and as Hall himself acknowledged in
publishing some of his own: "I know there is a store of sermons
extant: the pulpit scarce affordeth more than the press" (V, 1). Some
of the popularity and influence of the sermon can be attributed to
the religious contentiousness of the age, much to its love of rhetoric,
more than can be fully determined to the genius of individual
preachers. However the influence is explained, as Douglas Bush
observed, "It is hardly possible to exaggerate the importance of the
sermon in the seventeenth-century world."[3]

I Sermon Form

In Hall's day the sermon was considered a species of rhetoric,
fashioned by rules of form and style.[4] The great preachers of the
106

Patristic Age, many of whom like Augustine had been students and professors of rhetoric, had modeled their sermons on the classical oration, a formal composition whose parts, argumentative strategies, and style had been codified in the treatises of Cicero and Quintilian. Homiletic manuals of the sixteenth and seventeenth centuries preserved the tradition of constructing sermons along the lines prescribed by classical rhetoric; and, although allowing for the special proportion of the sermon as sacred discourse, they endorsed the use of the traditional figures and tropes in achieving the two main purposes of the sermon, scriptural exegesis and moral exhortation.

Hall, like other preachers of the Anglican school, followed traditional procedures. His first task in composing a sermon was the selection of a scriptural verse to "prove" his theme. This choice was normally governed by the liturgical season, sometimes by the identity of his audience or by the rubrics of the *Book of Common Prayer*, which cited verses appropriate to times of public celebration, penitence, or thinksgiving. Having "set" his text, Hall would then divide it into parts, taking clauses, phrases, or individual words of the verse as themes. Such division served to make the meaning of the verse plain and to provide the sermon with a table of contents, which Hall then followed scrupulously.

An example of Hall's sermon construction is "Wickedness Making a Fruitful Land Barren," preached before King James at Whitehall, 8 August 1624. Hall's text is Psalms 107: 34: "He turneth a fruitful land into barrenness for the wickedness of them that dwell therein"; his theme, that destruction follows the wicked. Hall begins the sermon by dividing his text as might a logician, according to the several aspects of the action described. Since every act presupposes an agent, and an agent a motive, Hall proceeds from effect to cause to determine the three heads of his discourse: "These three then must be the measure of my tongue and your ears; the change, the author, the merit" (V, 231). Having established the three major divisions of his sermon, he then proceeds to subdivision. The change—barrenness—is Hall's subject. He deals first with mutability as a universal principle, in the heavens, the elements, the sea and earth, and in commonwealths. When he turns to the second of his topics, he makes his transition emphatic: "This much for the subject and terms of this change: the agent follows; He turneth." All barrenness proceeds from a cause; upon this rule, he organizes the next section of the sermon. He first deals with secondary causes (e.g. adverse climate, wars, poor husbandry, plagues), then with primary (God's displeasure at the wicked). Another transitional paragraph signals his move to the third head: "Hitherto the agent: now follows the meriting cause of this change—*the wickedness of them that dwells therein*" (V, 241). Sterility is a punishment, and punishment is the consequence of sin. Around this principle Hall organizes this final section of his sermon. Briefly, he surveys the major ills of society: false security in worldly goods, oppression of the poor, contempt for the Church, and sacrilege. In summation, Hall exhorts his audience to fear God, that His judgments may be averted and the land be made fruitful.

While this is not the best of Hall's sermons, none shows more clearly his habitual manner of putting them together. Nor were Hall's methods in any way unique. The seventeenth century viewed the sermon as an argument; its divisions were considered the building blocks of a thesis, each sentence a discrete proof. Strict construction evidenced the preacher's learning and preparation, without which the sermon would have been, in effect, less cogent and the preacher seemingly less professional. Moreover, tidy organizing helped the preacher to memorize his text, and his audience to remember it. Hall's analytic approach to the scriptural verse was also *de rigeur* among the learned clergy who, trained in Ramist logic at Cambridge or Oxford, did not hesitate to apply the lessons of that rigorous discipline to the opening of God's word. Thus the art of the sermon required all of the preacher's intellectual power as well as the full measure of his religious fervor.

II   *Sermon Themes*

As a preacher, Hall had little interest in resolving knotty paradoxes or interpreting difficult passages of scripture. His was not a philosophical temperament, and unlike some of his learned colleagues, he did not approach the Bible as a *mysterium*, but as a settled, consistent, and ultimately clear revelation of the Divine Will. His passion was not speculation but the edification of his fellows. In his sermons, therefore, scriptural exegesis is always incidental to what he clearly feels his main charge: the application of scriptural teaching to the moral lives of his hearers. As he observes in one sermon, "Without any curious traversing of opinions, I study for simple truth; as one that will not lead you out of the roadway to show you the turnings" (V, 3).

Hall's themes include the principles of divinity, the Christian virtues, the need for repentance, and the nature and consequences of sin. Yet although Hall's orthodoxy prompted him to deal with general Christian issues, some themes deserve special notice, both because they recur and because they illustrate the essential conservatism of his world view. These are (1) the moral degeneration of the age, (2) the relation of private virtue to civic responsibility, and (3) the necessity of order in political and ecclesiastical affairs.

Hall's theology assumed man's natural depravity. As he put it in one sermon, "We are all too much the true son of our great grandmother, and have each of us an Eve's sweettooth in our head." Like many thoughtful men of his age—including his friend John Donne, who in his *Anniversaries* on the death of Elizabeth Drury expressed the idea most eloquently—Hall believed that his age was in a spiritual decline. Censuring his contemporaries as a "monstrous generation" and a "cold and hallow age," Hall found symptoms of degeneration in what he felt to be growing indifference to religion and a decline in morals. Of greatest complaint in this latter category were public drunkenness, the use of tobacco, and the behavior of gallants at court. Especially offensive to him as a sign of the times was the confusion of sexual roles, a theme he touched upon in a sermon preached on Easter Week 1618:

Whither doth the conceit of a little inheritance transport the gallants of our time? O God, what a world of vanity hast thou reserved us to! I am ashamed to think that the gospel of Christ should be disgraced with such disguised clients. Are they Christians, or antics in some carnival, or children's puppets, that are thus dressed? (V, 131)

He was hardly less vexed at the women:

Who can without indignation look upon the prodigies which this misimagination produces in that other sex; to the shame of their husbands, the scorn of religion, the damnation of their own souls? Imagine one of our forefathers were alive again, and should see one of these gay daughters walk in Cheapside before him; what do you think he would think it were? Here is nothing to be seen but a fardingale, a yellow ruff, and a periwig with perhaps some feathers waving in the top; three things for which he could not tell how to find a name. Sure he could not but stand amazed to think what new creature the times had yielded since he was a man: and if then he should run before her, to see if by the foreside he might guess what it were, when his eyes should meet with a powdered frizzle, a painted hide shadowed with a fan not more painted, breasts displayed, and a loose lock erring wantonly over her shoulders, betwixt a painted cloth and skin; how would he yet more bless himself to think what mixture in nature could be guilty of such a monster. (V, 131)

A more important evidence of modern degeneracy for Hall was social abuses. Of humble social origins himself, Hall had great sympathy for the poor. In a sermon preached at Paul's Cross, 1 May 1608, titled "Pharisism and Christianity," he contrasted the charity of earlier generations of Englishmen to that of the present generation, stripping the moral pretentions of those who professed themselves Christians but behaved as hypocritically as the Pharisees.

Woe to you, spiritual robbers! Our blind forefathers clothed the Church, you despoil it: their ignorant devotion shall rise in judgment against your ravening covetousness. If robbery, simony, perjury will not carry you to hell, hope still that you may be saved. They gave plentiful alms to the poor; we, instead of filling their bellies, grind their faces. (V, 12)

Although no social reformer, Hall was sensitive to economic injustice. In the same sermon, asserting that "every man would engross the whole world to himself," he complains against the courtiers who "grate upon poor trades with hard monopolies" and against merchants who load the poor with "deep and unreasonable prices, and make them pay dear for days." Nor were the gentry free from Hall's indictment: "Hence ye great men who wring the poor sponges of the commonality into your private purses, for the maintenance of pride and excess." And in a later sermon ("The True Peacemaker," 19 September 1624), noting ironically that it is the way of the world to find the censurer overly severe rather than the offender culpable, Hall provides his hearers—this time the court of James—with a survey of social ills, one of which, the enclosing of arable land for pasture, was most detestable to Hall. And in still another sermon ("The Fashions of the World") Hall returned to his theme in condemning "immoderate fees of lawyers, unreasonable prices in merchants, exactions in officers, oppression in landlords, encroachments in neighborhood, falsehood in servants and, lastly, cozenages in all sorts" (V, 290).

To Hall, a remedy for social ills was the good example of the ruling class, whose private virtues he considered essential in promoting similar virtues among the commons. He also insisted that only good men could make good subjects and, therefore, that moral rectitude was essential to an orderly society. In one sermon, for example, he asserts that "a lewd man can no more be a good subject than an ill subject can be a good man" (V, 229) and proceeds to upbraid those who believe that private evils have no public consequences. Convinced that God is swift to punish nations as well as individuals for impiety and wrongdoing, he sought to call the upper classes of his society to repentance, not only for their salvation but for the maintenance of political order.

Such was Hall's theme in a sermon preached before the Parliament, 18 February 1628/9. On this occasion—Ash Wednesday, a day of fasting and penitence—Hall took as his text Acts 2:37–40, Peter's injunction to the Jews to repent, be baptized, and save themselves from an "untoward generation." Like his "Pharisism and Christianity," preached two decades before, Hall's sermon to Parliament is a stern warning to a morally dissolute age. Here, however, Hall's concern was not hypocrisy, but the false assumption that good intentions and public service can compensate for wickedness. Concentrating on the key phrase of the verse, "untoward generation," Hall anatomizes moral corruption with resonant catalogues of enormities common to his age and the repetition of the question "What is an untoward generation?" that serves the sermon as a kind of refrain. Hall was not only concerned to anatomize evil, but to call the Parliament to repentance; for they are leaders of the nation in matters religious as well as political. The socially prominent have a responsibility beyond that of the ordinary Christian:

Hardly are those sins redressed that are taken up by the great; easily are those sins diffused that are warranted by great examples. The great lights of heaven, the most conspicuous planets, if they be eclipsed, all the almanacks of all nations write of it; whereas the small stars of the galaxy are not heeded. All the country runs to a beacon on fire; nobody regards to see a shrub flaming in a valley. Know then, that your sins are so much greater than yourselves are; and all the comfort that I can give you, without your true repentance is, "that mighty men shall be mightily tormented . . . So shall you help to save your nation from the imminent judgments of our just God. (V, 424)

Hall's love of order and reverence for authority are also prominent themes in his sermons. Most evident is his absolute faith in monarchical government, in the hierarchical order of the English Church, and in the divine authority of Scripture. "Monarchy is the best of governments, and likest to His rule that sits in the assembly of gods " (V, 93), Hall affirmed in a sermon preached at Paul's Cross on the tenth anniversary of James' inauguration. Another sermon, "Christ and Caesar," delivered at Hampton Court during the reign of Charles, is wholly devoted to defending the legitimacy of kingly authority in a Christian state. Not only is monarchy compatible with true religion, but Hall argues that "it is religion that teacheth us that God hath ordained kingly sovereignty," that "the same power which ordained Caesar enjoins all faithful subjection to Caesar, *not for fear but for conscience*," and that "Christ is not Caesar's rival, but Caesar's Lord and Patron" (V, 335). Referring to the insidious notion that religion was devised to keep men in awe, Hall concludes that it is religion, not craft, that is the firmest base for the state: "Let the great Caesars of the world then know, that the more subject they are to Christ, the more sure they are of the loyalty of their subjects to them. Neither is there in all the world any so firm and strait bond to tie the hearts of their people to them as true religion to God" (V, 335).

Corollary to Hall's reverence for order was his dislike of factionalism, especially in religion. That Rome was in error he took as a fundamental principle, and he loved to comment satirically on Papist practice he thought mere superstitious nonsense. But the division of the Reformed Churches into warring parties he found ominous, both because of its threat to civil peace and because of its defiance of Christ's injunction that his followers should be one in doctrine. Most grievous to Hall was the spirit of contention which permitted questions he felt not fundamental to Christian faith to become causes of deep division and political discord. Such was his objection to the Brownists in the early years of the century. Such, later, was his quarrel with the Puritans. Difference of opinion on matters "indifferent" he could tolerate; not so the distemper of zeal by which the extreme members of that party found a separation from the established Church and even exile the logical conclusion of their zeal. Hall addressed himself to this problem in a sermon preached before King Charles at Whitehall in 1641. On this occasion, Hall took as his text a verse from the Psalms: "Thou has made the earth to tremble; thou has broken it; heal the breaches thereof for it shaketh." His theme is specifically the mischief of factionalism and its causes; his strategy an extended analogy between literal earthquakes—a phenomenon only partly understood and greatly disconcerting to his contemporaries and civil disorder. Hall's point is that both are contrary to nature, both caused by subterraneous tremors:

I remember Georgius Agricola, who when I was a young man was noted for the most accurate observer of these underground secrets of nature, tells us, most probably, that the secondary and immediate cause of an earthquake is a certain subterraneous fire, kindled of some sulphureous matter within the bowels of that vast body, and increased by the resistence of the ambient coldness: the passages whereof being precluded and blocked up by the solid and cold matter of the earth, it rages and roars within those dark hallows; and by the violence of it, as murmuring to be thus forcibly imprisoned, shakes the parts about it, and at last makes way by some dreadful Vesuvian-like eruption. Such is the kindled heat of some vehement spirits; this, when it lights upon some earthy, proud, sullen, headstrong disposition, and finds itself crossed by an authoritative resistance; grows desperately unruly, and, in a mad indignation to be suppressed, is ready to shake the very foundations of government; and at last breaks forth into some dangerous rupture, whether in church or state. (V, 504–5)

To an audience for whom earthquakes were unnatural and fearsome, Hall's carefully worked out analogy could only have been most impressive. Hall is careful to point out that his criticism is not of a "wise, holy, well-governed zeal" but of the "unruly tempers of malcontented persons, and of the furies of anabaptism and separation" (V, 505). These, "like a colick in the guts," make ill the whole body politic. Those who cause civil disorder, Hall explains, are worse then murderers, for the evil they do is more infectious.

After citing numerous historical and biblical examples of civil broils caused by contentious persons, Hall suggests that since the source of rebellion is the disordered heart, each man must examine his own; and because holy affections can rule the heart as God's providence governs the natural order (and by extension, earthquakes) so does the love of God create a peaceful disposition. Hall concludes his sermon with an appeal for tolerance:

"This man is right," ye say; "that man is not right: this sound, that rotten."
And how so, dear Christians? What! for ceremonies and circumstances, for
rochets, or rounds, or squares? Let me tell you, he is right that hath a right
heart to his God, what forms soever he is for. The kingdom of God doth not
stand in meats and drinks: in stuffs or colours or fashions; in noises or
gestures; it stands in holiness and righteousness; in godliness and charity; in
peace and obedience; and if we have happily attained unto these, God doth
not stand upon trifles and niceties of indifferences; and why should we? (V,
517)

Hall was greatly disturbed by attacks on the authority of the
clergy and the scripture. Carrying out the Reformation ideal of
every man his own priest to its logical conclusion, the English dissenters denied the sole right of the clergy to interpret scripture and
to act as spiritual overseers. They claimed to receive special revelation or dared to advance mere speculation as sound doctrine. Much
of this, Hall believed, was rooted in an unhealthy love of novelty:
"the disease of the latter times, that now is grown epidemical; an
itch after news, even in God's chair; new doctrines, new dresses"
(V, 202). Hall held as fundamental the prerogative of the priesthood
to deal with questions of divinity. As he complained in a sermon
preached in 1628, "Wherefore serve universities, if every blue
apron may at his pleasure turn licentiate of divinity; and talk of
theological questions, which he understands not, as if they were to
be measured by the ell" (V, 419). In another, of the same year, Hall
expressed his distaste even more forcefully:

There is an audacious and factious liberty of this loose film [i.e. tongue],
which not only illtutored scholars take to themselves under the name of
libertas prophetandi, pestering both presses and pulpits with their bold and
brainsick fancies; but unlettered tradesmen, and tattling gossips too; with
whom deep questions of divinity, and censures of their teachers, are grown
into common table-talk; and peremptory decisions of theological problems
is as ordinary as backbiting their neighbors. (V, 394)

In all of this, Hall thought he heard the tearing of the fabric of his
society. Even in 1628 he was not far from wrong.

   The sermons of Hall's later years reflect indirectly the turbulence
of the times in their avoidance of controversial topics. During his
sequestration, he was allowed to preach; but Hall judiciously re-
frained from publicly condemning Cromwell or the Puritan regime,

although there could have been little doubt as to where his sympathies lay. Instead, he turned more to the inner life of the Christian, preaching on topics of general interest. Titles of his last published sermons reflect this tendency: "The Mourner in Zion," "Life a Sojourning," "Good Security." In "Life a Sojourning," preached to the little congregation of Higham, his place of exile, the year before his death, Hall seemed to be speaking of his own condition in enjoining his hearers to fortitude in the face of the world's "unkind and churlish entertainment":

Are we spitefully entreated by unjust men, our reputation blemished, our profession slandered, our goods plundered, our estates causelessly impaired, our bodies imprisoned, and all indignities cast upon us and ours? Let us bethink ourselves where and what we are; strangers and sojourners here: and let us make no reckoning to fare any otherwise while we sojourn in this vale of tears. (V, 650)

III   *Sermon Style*

Hall's sermons belong to that fashion of homiletics best classified as middle-Anglican.[5] Unlike the Puritans with whom he had certain affinities of temperament, he did not scorn the learning of the Fathers or reject the quotation of classical authorities; and unlike the Metaphysical preachers such as Donne and Andrewes, he did not strain for effect, overload his sermons with recherché learning, even though his scholarship was in some ways superior to Donne's and the equal of Andrewes'.[6] Like other learned clergymen of his party, Hall quoted from Latin, Greek, and Hebrew; pondered etymologies; cited the early Church Fathers, especially St. Augustine and St. Bernard; and showed a ready acquaintance with the polemical literature of his age. He thought, however, of his own sermon style as plain, believing that "beauty is, like truth, never so glorious as when it goes plainest" (V, 132); and, indeed, the modern reader will puzzle over twenty knotty passages in Donne or Andrewes before stumbling over one of Hall's.

The prose style of Hall's sermons is like that of his prose in general: sentences of "short sound, but large extent" (V, 174), simple diction, frequent use of proverb and aphorism, commonplace metaphors and images, and of course the extensive use of balance and antithesis, the characteristic features of his syntax. We miss the intense introspection of Donne or the poetic flashes of Taylor, but

Hall is quite capable, as we have already seen in this chapter, of a striking phrase; and not the least remarkable quality of his sermon style is a vividness of description by which he hoped to make his audience feel the force of his words.

Although as a preacher Hall did not seek to sear his audiences with the prospect of hellfire and damnation, he was capable of dramatizing the horrors of war and plague to remind them of the blessings of peace and health. In a sermon preached in 1613, for example, he presented his hearers with an impression of war's suffering and cruelty no less remarkable for its concreteness of detail than for the fact that its composite images almost surely came second hand from his reading or from conversation with returned soldiers.

O, my dear breathren, we never knew what it was to hear the murdering pieces about our ears; to see our churches and houses flaming over our heads; to hear the fearful cracks of their fall, mixed with the confused outcries of men, killing, encouraging to kill or resist, dying, and the shriekings of women and children: we never saw tender babes snatched from the breasts of their mothers, now bleeding upon the stones or sprawling upon the pikes, and the distracted mother ravished ere she may have leave to die. We never saw men and horses lie wallowing in their mingled blood, and the ghastly visages of death deformed with wounds; the impotent wife hanging with tears on her armed husband, as desirous to die with him with whom she may not live; the amazed runnings to and fro of those that would fain escape if they knew how, and the furious pace of a bloody victor. (V, 108–9)

Equally impressive are Hall's descriptions of the plague that struck London and its environs in 1625, an event he personally witnessed and which he relates in a sermon on public thanksgiving for the plague's abatement the same year:

What could we hear but alarms of death? What could we see but trophies of death? Here was nothing but groaning, and crying, and dying, and burying. Carts were the biers, wide pits were the graves, men's clothes were their coffins, and the very exequies of friends were murderous. The carcasses of the dead might say with the sons of the prophets, *Behold the place where we lie is too strait for us.* New dormitories are brought for the dead, and furnished. Neither might the corpses be allowed to lie single in their earthen beds, but are piled up like fagots in a stack for the society of the future resurrection. No man survived, but he might say with the Psalmist, that *thousands fell at his side, and ten thousands at his right hand.* And if we take all together, the mother and the daughters, surely the number was not much short of David's though his time were shorter. (V, 259)

As a preacher, Hall was conscious of the imaginative limitations of his hearers. His words do not merely evoke ideas, but images. For example, in a sermon preached at Higham, Easter Day, 1648, he vivified the idea of sin by comparing it to gangrene: "You see how a gangrene, even from the least toe, soon strikes the heart; and the canker, from a scarce sensible beginning, consumes the gums, eats through the cheek, eats down the nose; and will admit of no limits but deformity and death" (V, 602).

Like the lively image, the homely example served Hall well as a device of style. Hall never kept himself aloof from the concerns or experiences of common men. He had a knowledge of men and things, and his sermons are full of references to the work, tools, furnishings, and sights, smells, and sounds of city streets or country lanes. He seems to have had a basic knowledge of medicine, and to have known something about fencing and other sports. As a preacher he was ready to incorporate any impression of the eye, ear, nose, or mind into his message. We have seen how skillfully he turned his early reading of Georgius Agricola's treatise on earthquakes into an impressive analogy between tremors of the earth and political discord. With equal facility, he made ordinary experiences do yeoman service as moral analogues, as in this passage from a "Salvation from an Untoward Generation":

If we come into a field that hath some good plenty of corn, and store of weeds, though it be red with poppy, or yellow with carlock, or blue with wild-bottles or scabious, we still call it a cornfield; but if we come into a barnfloor, and see some few grains scattered amongst an heap of chaff, we do not call it a cornheap, the quantity of the offal devours the mention of those insensible grains. (V, 414)

Not the least notable aspect of Hall's style is prose rhythm, the ebb and flow of language. Hall's sermons, it is important to remember, are speeches; while all of Hall's prose can be read aloud, only his sermons were expressly so to be rendered. If, therefore, he was anywhere in his writing concerned for the compatibility of sounds, the march of a line, and the sweep of a paragraph it was in his sermons, whose success depended not only on engaging the mind of his hearers, but entrancing their ears.

While Senecanism is not usually associated with oratory, its characteristic preference for the loose sentence did produce a rhythm that came much closer to that of natural speech than did the Ciceronian periods with their conspicuous inversions and complicated construction. What is appealing about the rhythm of Hall's sermons is that we seem to hear a man speaking. The rhythm of natural speech is, of course, hard to define. Getting it right has something to do with the ordering of words in a sentence, the length and shape of its members, and the compatibility of all of these with the syntactic and phonetic features of neighboring sentences. At his best Hall writes not by the sentence (an impression often given by stylists of the Senecan school) but by the paragraph, so that while his sentences are terse and pointed, he also achieves continuity of sound as well as sense as he moves from the first word of the paragraph to the last. Hall's control of prose cadence gives his prose a suppleness that can not only accommodate a variety of tones and thus serve a variety of rhetorical aims, but also allow occasional departures from Senecan terseness.

The passage below, for example, from "Wickedness making a fruitful land barren," is a congregate of short clauses welded into a continuous movement of sound:

Thus, when the fair face of the earth shall be turned from a youthful and flourishing greenness into a parched and withered deformity; the leaves, which are the hairs, fall off, and give way to a loathsome baldness; the towered cities, which are the chaplets and dresses of that head, are torn down, and turned to rubbish; the fountains and rivers, which are the crystalline humours of those eyes, are dried up; the surface, which is the skin of that great body, is chopped and chinked with drought, and burnt up with heat; those sweet waters of heaven, and those balmy drops of fatness wherewith it was wont to be besprinkled, are restrained, and have given place to unwholesome sereness and killing vapours; shortly, that pampered plenty, wherewith it was glutted, is turned into a pinching want: this change is not more sensible than woful. (V, 235)

The passage is in every way typical in the masterly control of sound and momentum it exhibits. Most evident, of course, is the parallelism, rigid enough for poise, free enough for variety. We observe how carefully "parched and withered deformity" echoes "youthful and flourishing greenness," how the "whiches" and "wherewiths" form an orderly file and how the placing of those clauses, in apposition, so that the speaker must pause and lower the voice to another register for emphasis, retards the flow of the sentences, preventing the short sentences from rushing to their conclusion at an undignified pace. There is alliteration, but not too much; and the terminal clause, defying its fellows in brevity and in simplicity, punctuates the paragraph.

To his contemporaries, Hall was a powerful preacher of the Word, and like his other literary endeavors, his sermons set a standard for their kind. Bishop Hall's "way" was one of five sermon styles represented in Abraham Wright's *Five Sermons,* a manual of preaching published in 1656. We may suppose that Wright's use of Hall as a model reflects faithfully not only Hall's contemporary reputation but also his leadership of the "schematic" or "rhetorical" school of sermon writers.

For moderns, Hall's sermons, as Mitchell observed, are full of beautiful and arresting effects. We do not write now so schematically, but we may still appreciate the intricacy of his patterns, the almost Prussian tidiness of his periods; for it is in his style that Hall, in so many other ways conservative, even reactionary, for his times, was ahead of them in the extraordinary lucidity of his prose. What he, with characteristic modesty, once called his "poor and plain fashion" was a prophesy of things to come.[7]

CHAPTER 7

The Middle Way

HALL was well known for his moderation, a quality of mind evident in his service at the Council of Perth, the Synod of Dort, and in the perilous middle road he traveled as priest and bishop between Laud's high-church Anglicanism and radical Puritanism. A gentle man, he disliked religious broils, yet he never remained aloof from them, believing that the battle for truth was also a war against error. If therefore, as he often protested, he had little heart for contention, he did have sufficient stomach for polemics, for so may many of his works be classed. Only marginally literature, they are a practical sort of prose, written not for the ages but for the moment. Hall's polemical writings have many literary qualities, however, and much historical value. Whether directed against Pope or Puritan, they reveal the impression seventeenth-century Anglicanism had of itself and the polemic art of one of its most able defenders.

I   *Hall vs. Rome*

Hall's anti-Papistical writings—a handful of tracts and epistles— express the general hostility of the Anglican community toward the church from which it had divorced itself a century before. With Hooker, the greatest of Anglican writers, Hall found Rome errant in doctrine, corrupt and superstitious, and tyrannical in its pretense to universal authority. He was especially offended that by reason of their dogma, he and his Protestant countrymen were condemned as heretics, outside the pale of salvation. Yet Hall prosecuted his case against Papacy with less rancor than many of his coreligionists had done; for although English hatred of Roman Catholicism remained intense even into the seventeenth century, it was becoming in-

120

creasingly clear that whatever political danger a militant Papistry might represent, a militant Puritanism was even a greater threat to sound theology.[1]

Hall's *The Peace of Rome*, published in 1609, consisted of two parts: a short preface condemning those who desert to the Papists and an extended examination of three hundred points of doctrine on which learned Catholics disagreed. The reformed churches had often been charged with an inability to agree on fundamental issues; in *The Peace of Rome* (the title, of course, is ironic), Hall aimed to show Catholic unity a myth.[2] His strategy was to cull from the writings of the chief Roman apologist of the age, Cardinal Bellarmine, evidence of Catholicism's own internal conflicts; yet however this may have strengthened Hall's argument, it makes for a less interesting book. Reading *The Peace of Rome* is much like perusing an industrious student's notes. Hall divides his theme methodically among four decades or books, treating such topics as scriptural canon, the nature of the sacrament, and original sin, and he provides a useful index. Indeed, he is more editor than author, for he has himself little to say about the issues.

More interesting to the modern reader is Hall's *The Honour of the Married Clergy* (1620). Hall had handled this theme earlier in a three-page epistle to John Whiting (*Epistles, Second Decade*), composing both a sturdy defense of marriage and a trenchantly ironic attack on the Roman Church in which he lumped Papists with atheists and argued that enforced celibacy was as vicious as marriage lawful. In response to a critique of his epistle by a "C.E.," a Catholic priest, in this greatly expanded version Hall gave his polemical powers full scope. The compatibility of marriage and the priesthood was an issue Protestants and Catholics had fought long and hard over since the beginning of the Reformation. Hall, like other Protestants, did not deny that for those capable of it virginity represented a higher state than marriage ("The approbation and better experience of single life in capable subjects, we do willingly subscribe unto"), but he denied that marriage was incongruous with God's service or human sexuality inherently evil.[3] He argued, rather, that in marriage "the pravity of incontinence is ruled, and the fruitfulness of nature graced." This proposition he maintained with considerable erudition, quoting scriptures and Church fathers to prove that marriage was honorable and ancient, that the apostles enjoyed their wives while they enjoyed their apostleship, and that enforced celibacy was a novel doctrine instituted by men and not God. Since the work is oriented toward demolishing his Catholic critic as well as defending the sanctity of marriage, the general tedium of Hall's erudition is relieved by occasional flashes of wit, of which the opening sentence is typical: "Neither my charity, nor my leisure, not my reader's patience, will allow me to follow my detector in all his extravagances; not to change idle words of contumely with a babbler." Elsewhere in the tract Hall labels his adversary a "moody mass-priest" and "some sorry quib, that after a little hissing and sparkling ends in an unsavoury crack," and concludes that "C.E. hath accused much, and proved nothing; vaunted much, and done nothing; railed much, and hurt nothing; laboured much, and gained nothing; talked much, and said nothing."

For all his moderation, Hall was not adverse to dredging up old scandals about the incontinence of Roman priests. Since he believed marriage a natural and holy outlet for sexual passion, he could only conclude that when such an outlet was blocked, the passion must be expressed in unnatural ways ("Where the water is dammed up, and yet the stream runs full how can it choose but rise over the banks?") We are therefore treated, at least in part, to a vision of frustrated priests making their way to houses of ill fame, or, worse, to neighboring nunneries, a scenario congenial with Hall's impression of Italy as a sinkhole of vice.

In the most polished of his anti-Roman tracts, *The Old Religion* (1628), Hall clearly defined the differences in doctrine between the reformed and Catholic churches. Composed shortly before his creation as Bishop of Exeter, the work shows Hall bending his style "against" Popish doctrine with such Christian moderation, "as may argue zeal without malice; desire to win souls, no will to gall them." For the schism between Rome and the reformed churches Hall blamed Rome. Luther had pleaded for reform from within, but his plea had been rejected. The Roman communion, Hall insisted, was a particular, not a universal church, without the power to create fundamental articles of faith or declare as heretics those who disagreed with its bulls and councils. The book is topically arranged, with sections for major theological points such as transubstantiation, indulgences, and purgatory; and in each section Hall first defines the doctrine, then proves it contrary to scripture and reason. Hall had an orderly mind that lent itself to such cataloguing, and what

the treatise lacks in imagination and penetrating theological insight
it almost makes up for in its methodical inventory of Anglican objections to Roman dogma.

Convinced as he was of the truth of Tertullian's dictum, *primus
verus* (the first is truest), Hall was anxious to rebut the Roman
Catholic charge that Protestantism was novel by insisting that Papist
doctrines such as transubstantiation, purgatory, and justification by
works were of recent origin, developed in the face of scriptural
warrant. Anglicanism, on the contrary, represented for Hall, if not
quite a restoration of primitive Christianity, at least a theology more
harmonious with its teachings:

> Be it therefore known to all the world, that our church is only reformed or
> repaired, not made new. There is not one stone of a new foundation laid by
> us; yea, the old walls stand still; only the overcasting of those ancient stones
> with the untempered mortar of new inventions displeaseth us. (VIII, 643)

Although Hall surely felt he had put Papistry in its place in *The
Old Religion*, he had not done so to the satisfaction of some Puritans, for in the following year an "advertisement" to the readers of
his second edition began with the observation that "nothing can be
so well said or done, but may be ill taken." Hall's offense, from the
Puritan point of view, was that he had granted Rome to be a visible
church.[4] In his "advertisement" he reiterated the claim, explaining,
however, that true spirituality did not necessarily follow mere visi-
bility and that to call Rome a visible church was only to say that it
professed Christianity. He believed he had made it perfectly clear
that she practiced something quite different. Despite his clarifica-
tion—and an attempt to find support for his alleged "leniency" in
the writings of Hooker and other major Anglican writers—Hall to
the end of his life was accused of being "soft" on Rome by ardent
Puritans who never allowed the moderate stance of *The Old Religion* to be forgotten.

II   *Hall vs. the Brownists*

As a polemicist, Hall reserved his most severe rebuke for the
Puritan Separatists. His first foray against the sect was in an epistle
to John Smith and John Robinson, leaders of the Separatist colony in
Amsterdam. To this brief, but stinging, censure Smith and Robin-

son replied with a pamphlet attacking Hall and his party. The exchange provoked Hall's first full-scale polemic, *A Common Apology of the Church of England Against the Unjust Challenges of the Over-Just Sect Commonly Called Brownists* (1610).

Hall's *Apology* is a vigorous, point-by-point rebuttal of the Brownist pamphlet, with passages from the offending document quoted in Hall's text. In their retort, the Separatist leaders had accused Hall of being ignorant of the reasons for their exile and charged that the canons, morals, hierarchy and ordinances of the Established Church were corrupt. Since these accusations were those commonly levied against the English Church by the Puritans, Hall's purpose was not only to justify his epistle, but to present a coherent defense of the English reformation as a legitimate "separation" from Rome.

In many ways Hall's *Apology* is standard polemical fare. Like other controversialists, he matches his scriptural verses with those of his opponents, his authorities with theirs, and fleshes his argument out with biblical precedents, historical examples, and homely analogies. There is nothing in the substance of his rebuttal not earlier proferred by Whitgift, Jewel, or Hooker nor is his colloquial vigor unique. Hall's first virtue, however, was a logical mind; and it is the intellectual vitality of his argument, the evident zest with which he pounces on contradictions and tautologies, suddenly confronts his opponents with a dilemma, or artfully rubs their noses in the inconsistencies of their argument that makes his *Apology* entertaining as well as cogent. He ridicules the Brownist pretense to exclusive revelation ("Hath God spoken these things to you alone?") and, even more stingingly, what he considered the "novel singularity" of their doctrine ("What, all in all ages and places, till now apostates?"). He saves his most caustic rebuke for the disunity and confusion in the Separatist ranks, which he believed undermined their claims to doctrinal purity: "Nothing, say we, can be more disorderly than the confusion of your democracy; or popular state, if not anarchy: where all in a sort ordain and excommunicate" (IX, 19).

Hall's defense of the Anglican *via media* was essentially Hooker's.[5] The English Church is not the daughter of Rome but a sister; its origins are found in primitive Christianity; and its canons, while they may be common to Catholics, are not so derived. "Our Christian faith came not from the Seven Hills; neither was derived from Augustin the monk, or Pope Gregory. Britain had a worthy church before either of them looked into the world" (IX, 46). As a chaste sister, the English Church looks upon Rome as apostate and corrupt, yet still a visible church in so far as it holds to some tenets fundamental to the Christian faith. Puritans, on the other hand, err in confusing "things indifferent" such as modes of worship and church policy with things essential to faith, in believing scripture the sole source of religious authority, and in supposing these just grounds for separation and exile. Hall is quick to defend his church against the charges of moral corruption, admitting what he cannot deny, that as a society it incorporates the sinner as well as the saint, but insisting that this does not preclude its being a true church: "If there be disproportion and dislocation of some parts, is it no true human body? Will you rise from the feast, unless the dishes be set on in your own fashion? Is it no city, if there be mudwalls half broken, low cottages unequally built, no state-house?" (IX, 19) The ceremonies of the English Church Hall justifies on the grounds of their antiquity and of their utility as vehicles of "order, decency, convenience" (IX, 92).

Hall's terseness lent itself to debate, as did his fondness for aphorism. He did not wish to demolish the Separatists, as much as he detested their separation, but to whip them soundly and send them off with their tails between their legs. His main weapon was a mocking irony, echoing Puritan cant and exposing Puritan hypocrisy. Hall was fond of wordplay, and that can become tedious, as in his lengthy consideration of legitimate and illegitimate "separations." But the dominant impression of Hall's polemical style is vigor of mind and language.

III *Hall vs. the Presbyterians*

In 1638 the Bishop of Orkney resigned his bishopric and apologized for having accepted its honors at a conference of Scottish clergy in Edinburgh. This startling act, a symptom of growing resentment of episcopal power, provoked Hall's most important polemic, *Episcopacy by Divine Right* (1640).

Hall had a vested interest in the ecclesiastical status quo. He was by then Bishop of Exeter and by his own account, "setting foot over the threshold of the house of my age." But he was strongly opposed to Presbyterianism, on political as well as religious grounds. Presbyterianism, or church government by presbyters or elders, was a feature of the reformed churches of Holland and Geneva, a government Hall accepted as resulting from the direction the Reformation had taken in these two countries. England, however, was a monarchy; and its Reformation, while popularly supported, had come about through royal direction in a succession of edicts and proclamations. With his deep distrust of change and his equally profound devotion to monarchical government, Hall saw Presbyterianism as a threat to the state as well as to the church. Since episcopal government with its hierarchical order corresponded to the political structure of monarchy, the implied egalitarianism of Presbyterianism could only undermine civil authority and bring the chaos of democracy. For Hall, there was deep wisdom in King James' famous dictum, "No bishop, no King."

Hall's aim in *Episcopacy*, then, was to defend the rule of bishops and refute the Presbyterian position. This was no small charge. By the middle of the seventeenth century the Protestant Reformation had built up a powerful momentum that threatened to sweep away all vestiges of the old religion. Because episcopal dignities remained the single most conspicuous leftover of Roman Catholicism in the English Church, the bishops were the bugbear of extreme Puritan reformers, many of whom were clergymen and, like Hall, steeped in all the arts of rhetoric and logic. Among these was Robert Parker, whose *De Politae Ecclesiastici Christi*, published in Frankfort in 1616, was an eloquent defense of the Presbyterian position. Although Hall had more than Parker's work in mind when he wrote his treatise, it is to Parker that he most frequently refers.

Episcopacy is a formal treatise divided into three books. The first of these defends episcopacy on the basis of its antiquity, a strong plank to Hall's readers both because of their veneration for history and because the Presbyterians, like all Puritans, tended to resort to the practice of primitive Christianity for their rules of order and worship. Hall argued that since the rule of bishops was the first form of church government recorded in scripture it was reasonable to conclude that it was apostolic and therefore divinely instituted. This view he found seconded in the earliest Fathers, while the universal acceptance of bishops in Christian churches until recent times offered a sure clue to the falsity of rule by presbyters.

For some Presbyterians, episcopacy was merely an institution without scriptural warrant; for the more ardent spirits, it was tyrannical and unchristian. But neither group disputed the existence of bishops in the primitive church, and both were united in the convic-

tion that bishops constituted no separate and superior order. In
Book II, then, Hall moved to counter these arguments and prove
episcopal government both divine in origin and essential to the true
church. Since the quarrel centered largely on the interpretation of
scriptural evidence, Hall was first at pains to show that the hierarchical principle was evident from the beginning, offering as proof
Christ's elevation of the apostles to a position superior to other
ministers of the Word. He then proceeded to infer the nature of the
bishop's office from the epistles of Paul to Timothy and Titus, and
from the writings of the earliest Fathers, principally Ignatius and
others who give "large and full testimonies of the acknowledged
superiority of bishops, and of the high respects that are and ever
were due to these prime governors of the church" (IX, 225). Hall
prosecuted his case with his wonted vigor and clarity. His strategy
was to overwhelm the opposition with the sheer quantity of his
"proofs" and to cast in the teeth of modern critics of episcopacy the
reverend authority of the ancients:

I have dwelt long with blessed Ignatius: where could I find better? That one
author is instead of many. Why should I not boldly say, if, besides the
divine scriptures, there were no other testimony but this one saint's, it were
abundant enough to carry this cause; and I must wonder at any man, who
confessing Ignatius to have been so holy a bishop, so faithful a martyr, so
true a saint, can stick at a truth, so often, so confidently, so zealously
recommended by him to the world. For me, let my soul go with his: let his
faith be mine: and let me rather trust one Ignatius then ten thousand
Cartwrights, Parkers, Ameses, or any other of their ignorant and malcon-
tended followers. (IX, 226)

   Since the formal polemic required that the polemicist refute the
opposition as well as sustain his own thesis, in his final and shortest
book Hall turned his attention to the lay presbyter, an office he
found unauthorized by scripture, unsupported by tradition, and
ridiculous in conception, offering as it did the prospect of mechanics
and tinkers meddling in matters far above their capacities. On this
last point, Hall was especially firm:

Can it therefore be possible, in such a kingdom as our happy England is,
where there are thousands of small village parishes . . . for every parish to
furnish an ecclesiastical consistory, consisting of one or more pastors, a
doctor, elders, decons? Perhaps there are not so many houses as offices are

required. And whom shall they then be judges of? And some of these so far remote from neighbors, that they cannot participate of their either teaching or censure: and if this were feasible, what stuff would there be! Perhaps a young indiscreet giddy pastor: and for a doctor, who and where, and what? John a Nokes and John a Stiles the elders! Smug the Smith a deacon! And whom or what should these rule, but themselves and their ploughshares? (IX, 269)

But although Hall could laugh at the idea of lay control of church affairs, the alternative to episcopal government presented by his opponents obviously caused him more often to shudder than deride; for in a time when religious authority was a basis of political power, what he jestingly calls "lawless Polycorany" where "every parish minister and his eldership should be a bishop and his consistory; yea a pope and his conclave of cardinals within his own parish, not subject to controllment, not liable to superior censure," was a threat to political order as well as an affront to Deity. Hall's temperate call to his readers in the final pages of his treatise to reason and obedience reflects his awareness of how serious a threat to civil peace was this squabble over church government.

IV   The Smectymnuan Controversy and Milton

Hall's learned apology won applause at court and among his fellow churchmen but quickly drew fire, first from a group of nonconformist clergymen writing under the acronym, "Smectymnuus," then from an even more formidable opponent, John Milton. To this controversy belong *An Humble Remonstrance to the High Court of Parliament* (January 1640–1), *a Defence of the Humble Remonstrance* (April 1641), and *A Short Answer to the Tedious Vindication of Smectymnuus* (August 1641). A fourth pamphlet, *A Modest Confutation of Animadversions* (1642), although attributed to Hall, was probably written by his son.

On 8 November 1641, the English Parliament issued to its sovereign, Charles I, what came to be called the "grand remonstrance," citing abuses in church and state during his reign and calling for reform. The document specifically called for depriving the bishops of their vote in the House of Lords and for granting special privileges to the Puritans, who then virtually controlled the lower house. The document was accepted and on 1 October Charles received the petition. Hall's *Humble Remonstrance*, published several months afterward, was a defense of episcopal privilege. Because Charles refused in any meaningful way to respond to Parliament's demands, London was in an uproar, and petitions calling for the abolition of bishop's rule were freely circulated in the city. Hall's *Humble Remonstrance* was both an answer to the "grand remonstrance" of Parliament and a response to the turbulent state of affairs among the London citizenry.

Hall's pamphlet, like Milton's *Areopagitica*, is a classical oration, adhering strictly to traditional rules of form and style. From its suasive beginning *(exordium)* to its conciliatory last words *(peroratio)* Hall was concerned to lay open before the highest tribunal of his land an essay in accord with the highest standards of eloquence. His argument defended the legitimacy of episcopal government and the Anglican liturgy and refuted two misconceptions: that he and other bishops had switched their defense of episcopacy from royal prerogative to divine right and that by claiming episcopacy a divine institution they had condemned reformed churches without such government. To maintain his thesis, Hall fell back on his old arguments, the sanction of authority and tradition, the "ill-advised newfangledness" of Presbyterianism, and Hooker-like sentiments: "right reason and sound experience inform us, that things indifferent or good, having been by continuance and general appropriation well rooted in church or state, may not upon light grounds be pulled up" (IX, 288). This was, of course, nothing more than *Episcopacy by Divine Right* in a nutshell. Yet Hall's refutation is more interesting because it expresses clearly his idea of the relationship of church and state and because it suggests the extent to which he was prepared to go to mediate between his own faction and the Presbyterians. There was little difference, he argued, between God's act and the King's in the creation of bishops. "It is the King that gives the bishopric; it is God that makes the bishop." God thus calls the bishop to his office, while civil authority grants him the right to exercise it and to execute those duties involving church government. As to the charge that in positing the divinity of episcopacy the Established Church was illegitimatizing nonepiscopal churches, Hall had this distinction to make:

Every church therefore which is capable of this form of government [i.e. episcopal] both may and ought to affect it, as that which is with so much authority derived from the apostles to the whole body of the church upon earth; but those particular churches to whom this power and faculty is denied lose nothing of the true essence of a church, though they miss something of their glory and perfection, whereof they are barred by the necessity of their condition; neither are liable to any more imputation in their credit and esteem than an honest, frugal, officious tenant, who, notwithstanding the proffer of all obsequious services, is tied to the limitations and terms of an hard landlord. (*Works*, IX, 291)

Hall's careful distinction between "essence" and "perfection" was lost on his nonconforming opponents, as the sequel to the controversy shows; but it is hard to see how anyone could have taken offense at Hall's tone, which was as respectful, even reverent, and as conciliatory as one might wish. Indeed, Hall's polemic is replete with what we could today call the ecumenical spirit. The Parliament are wise judges; Hall's enemies good men misled. "We are all," he insists in closing, "true breathren. We are one with you both in heart and brain, and hope to meet you in the same heaven" (IX, 295).

A *Defence of the Humble Remonstrance*, the sequel to Hall's oration, has less of the spirit of sweet reasonableness. When the *Humble Remonstrance* was no sooner published than attacked by a group of Presbyterian clergy writing under the acronym "Smectymnuus," Hall, shocked that his "meek and gall-less" discourse should have provoked such a caustic reply, responded in kind.

Hall's *Defense*, as long and tedious as the Smectymnuan *Answer*, is a closely argued rebuttal, lacking the stately eloquence of the *Humble Remonstrance* or the philosophical scope of the earlier tracts. Now, as Hall was wont to say, he was really in the lists. Hall accused the Smectymnuans of deliberately misreading his remonstrance, an error of which they were surely guilty. As a result, he was once again obliged to sift scriptural evidence, to evoke patristic testimony, in order to prove the thesis he had supported for thirty years, the divine right of episcopacy. The misconstructions of the Smectymnuans drew him into a critique of Smectymnuan logic. Unlike his *Apology of the Church of England*, which extended beyond its immediate aim as refutation, the *Defense* bogged down in a line by line critique, the analysis of faulty syllogisms, and a haggling over terms and translations. All produced an intellectual dryness that even Hall must have found wearisome.

Hall's *Short Answer* (July 1641) to the Smectymnuans' *Vindica-*

tion is cut from the same cloth. Closely argued and pedantic, it deals particularly with the Smectymnuan attacks on the liturgy and the practice of set prayers, viewed from the Puritan perspective as vestiges of Papistry and hindrances to true religion. Hall did not oppose the practice or deny the efficacy of "conceived" or spontaneous prayer. He admitted practicing it himself and insisted that in no orthodox canon was it forbidden. He did, however, insist on the efficacy of set forms, which he believed had not been instituted as a temporary help "in the want and the weakness of ministers," as the Smectymnuans argued, but as a perpetual aid to achieve the "uniformity of divine services in every national church; the opportunity of the better joining together of all hearts in common devotion; the better convenience of fixing the thoughts upon the matter of a foreknown expression" (IX, 429). Moreover, Hall insisted that set prayers, like episcopacy itself, were ancient and therefore of apostolic authorship, a position that led once again into the arid antiquarianism to which his love of history and reverence for tradition made him so easily a victim: "What can you say against the large Samaritan Chronicle which I produced, turned out of Hebrew into Arabic, written in a Samaritan character, and now not a little esteemed by the great and eminently judicious primate, in whose library it is?" (*Works* IX, 414)

But although Hall's scholarship was inexhaustible, his patience was not. In the Smectymnuan *Vindication* he clearly saw the redundancy that was the bane of the whole controversy. In responding to the Smectymnuan charge that his arguments for episcopacy and liturgy were "long since overworn, and beaten out, and baffled" he responded,

In good time, brethren! And why should not I take leave to return the same answer to you in this your tedious velitation of episcopacy? There is not one new point in this your overswoln and unwieldy bulk, No haycock hath been oftener shaken abroad, and tossed up and down in the wind, than every argument of yours hath been agitated by more able pens than mine: *Haic omnia jamdudum sunt protrita et profligata.* Why should I abuse my good hours, and spend my last age, devoted to better thoughts, in an unprofitable babbling? (IX, 442)

The Smectymnuans were no match for Hall. He bested them in his knowledge of scripture and church history, in his wide reading of contemporary religious literature, in his facility with ancient tongues.[6] His tempered but effective irony, the residue of his earlier practice as a satirist, put them down at every turn. John Milton, following the interchange with great interest, saw the Smectymnuans getting the worst of it and himself entered the lists in July, 1641 on their behalf.

Milton had already published two "anti-prelatical" tracts (On Reformation Touching Church Discipline in England and Of Prelatical Episcopacy) in 1641, and in his Animadversions upon the Remonstrant's Defence he heaped all the contempt he had for bishops in general on Hall in particular. The method of his tract was to cite and refute nearly 150 statements from Hall's Defence, but his Animadversions are not so much a rebuttal as a running commentary aimed at sending Hall off "well bespurted with his own holy water." Hall's weighty arguments from authority and tradition, Milton scorned as tedious and irrelevant: "I shall not intend this hot season to bid you the base through the wide, and dusty champaigne of the Councels." He focused rather on Hall's logical misdemeanors, his "spruce, fastidious oratory," and offhanded remarks of Hall's that were especially vulnerable to Milton's razor-sharp wit. Milton even recalled Hall's past as a satirist, in scathing allusions both to the Virgidemiae and the Mundus. Because of its form and Milton's tactics, the Animadversions is largely an exchange of quips and pedantries that do little credit to either author. There are purple passages in which Milton waxes eloquent on Episcopal skulduggery or apocalyptic visions of England's religious future, but these barely redeem page after page of nagging and carping. For example, to Hall's crack, "Wanton wits must have leave to play with their own stern," Milton rejoined, "A meditation of yours doubtless observed at Lambeth from one of the episcopal kittens"; and to Hall's assertion that "no one clergy in the whole Christian world yields so many eminent schollers, learned preachers, grave, holy and accomplished divines as the Church of England," Milton merely emitted a scornful laugh.

Milton justified the "rough accents" of his polemic by observing that enemies of truth deserved no less. But despite the intense animosity he displayed, it is clear that if he could not respect Hall as a bishop, he could as an opponent. Hall's real strengths as a polemicist—his literary skill and moderating stance—are indirectly acknowledged in Milton's preface, even though they are labeled as "a voluble and smart fluence of tongue" and a "wily strategem." As for Hall's alleged logical inadequacies, it is not clear that Milton was superior to Hall in choplogic. Both, in the heat of controversy, could misconstrue an argument or misshape a syllogism; both were quick to blame in others what they were guilty of themselves. As much as Hall's terse Senecanism clashed with Milton's opulent Ciceronian rhetoric, Milton saw in Hall's pen a real danger to the full reformation of church polity and practice to which he was so strongly committed.

Milton's tract set the tone for the sequel to the controversy. It was no sooner in print before an angry rejoinder was published, defending Hall's position and personally slandering Milton. Hall did not write *A Modest Confutation* (1642), although his son may have been its author, and it therefore forms no part of our story. It is enough to say that it provoked the last installment in the bitter controversy between Hall and Milton, Milton's *Apology Against . . . a Modest Confutation* in which Milton not only defended his education, his doctrine, and his chastity, but embellished, with great vituperation, his critique of Hall's theology and morals, taking casual shots at Hall's satires and ridiculing the style "of one who makes sentences by the statute, as if all above three inches long were confiscat."

How Hall weathered Milton's blast cannot be known. Certainly the gentle Bishop must have found it the bitter genesis of what he was later to call his "hard measure." Yet there is no little irony in their antagonism. As spokesmen for their respective parties, both were driven to magnify personal differences. To Milton, Hall was just another prelate, a canker on the church politic; to Hall, Milton was another rancorous Puritan who would not abide the dictates of reason and tradition. From an objective viewpoint, both Anglican and Puritan had much in common, not the least of which was their devotion to learning and strict personal piety.[7] In the fever of the moment, however, all sense of commonality was lost. To recognize the powerful ideological conflict that prevented their union as Christian brethren and would soon drive their nation to civil war is to go far toward forgiving whatever rancor or slander possessed either writer in the heat of controversy.

Hall was an able polemicist. His devotion to tradition, order, and reason brought him into sharp conflict with the more progressive thought of his time. Yet convinced of the rightness of his opinions, he defended them vigorously and articulately, mustering all his talents as rhetorician and scholar and often employing the poignant irony and witty sarcasm he had learned early as a satirist. As his theology sought to mediate between extremes, so did his polemical style seek a middle ground between bland exposition and vituperation. Thus, in an age when religious controversy was prone to querulousness, Hall's controversial writings are as moderate in stance as their author in temperament. As a polemicist he liked to appeal to reason, to extend the prospect of reconciliation to opponents he viewed not so much as enemies as misled brethren.

With his arrest and imprisonment in 1642, Hall's career as a polemicist ended. Thereafter he could offer up prayers, but not pamphlets, to the Anglican cause. Yet by the middle of the century the *via media* of Anglicanism was clearly defined and by the next generation firmly established. Hall had had no small part to play in that victory.

CHAPTER 8

Epilogue: The Mind of the Moralist

A N epilogue on the work of Joseph Hall should be brief after his own fashion, and it should be honest. Unlike some other authors of his time whose reputations have fluctuated with the critical seasons, Hall does not require a promotion. He is a writer of the second rank, dedicated, competent, and in some ways innovative and even "important." He does not need, in a word, to be rediscovered, but his efforts do need to be seen in reasonable perspective.

First to be considered is his matter, what Henry James calls the author's "given." Hall's writings fill ten volumes, twelve in one edition. They deal with his views on morals, personal and societal, church government (and hence by implication politics), and the spiritual life. We can quarrel with the author's "given"—although James encouraged us not to—but if the least that can be said of Hall's authorship is that it was prolific, the worst that can be maintained of his opinions is that they were commonplace. Scholars have thus deplored openly the unoriginality of Hall's conceptions (lamenting secretly perhaps that he did not, like Milton, write epics or, like DeLoney, write novels), even while commending his style.

But whatever inference may be drawn about the limitations of Hall's mind from the unoriginality of his principles, those limitations seem largely to have followed from his moralizing temper. He had a passion for instruction, and holding as he did to a traditional Christian theology, he can hardly be blamed for valuing most highly such conduct that accorded with salvation of the soul or believing that leading men to it was worth his best efforts as an author. He was a sober man, his satirical proclivities notwithstanding, given to quiet reflection on ordinary events and objects, and trusting, as had Hooker, in the security of what had in so many times and places been believed. As to the unoriginality that haunts all moralists, C. S. Lewis has this to say: "It is doubtful whether any moralist of

135

unquestioned greatness has ever attempted more (or less) than the defense of the universally acknowledged."[1] For originality—or at least our modern notion of it—Hall in any case would have cared little. Moral precepts, he would have insisted, proceed from God's word, not from fallen reason, which can only aspire to the austere but pitiable bravery of Stoicism. Demanding of Hall then the creativity of a speculative philsopher is very much like damning apples for tasting too little like oranges.

Hall is most fairly judged within the self-acknowledged scope of his endeavor, the articulation of received ideas in a variety of literary forms and in a suitable style. Hall's status as a pioneer in a handful of prose types has been widely recognized, and it is in no way to his discredit if we discover that some of these types were not so much invented by him as exhumed from the classical repertory. He should not lose the honor of discovery merely because in retrospect it seems easy to have accomplished or because its connection with his school exercises seems obvious. Hall was, as Douglas Bush has noted, "one of the most versatile and experimental of literary clerics."[2] If it cannot be demonstrated that he changed the course of literary history, it can be said that he broadened its expanse, leaving an amplitude for greater men and women to fill.

As a stylist, Hall made an equally important, if somewhat less conspicuous, contribution. For Hall, style was a preoccupation, not merely because he loved artifice but because he was committed to ideals of order and clarity, qualities he equated with ethical rectitude and theological truth. He was not a Puritan but he shared their love for plainness. Whether the word was God's or reason's, its presentation was a moral act; communication required a translucency of style that permitted the matter to take center stage, to be memorable, and to be understandable. Thus Hall's fondness for aphorism and the rhetorical mechanics by which he achieved it—concinnity, parallelism, and antithesis—were subsumed in a moral philosophy that, like Bacon's, prized matter above manner. We shape our sentences differently now, but certainly we write more after Hall's fashion than Donne's or Browne's or Milton's. Perhaps, paradoxically, it is the very triumph of the Senecan style that obscures its lasting influence on English prose. Hall is therefore one of those unusual literary figures who, rooted in the past, nonetheless anticipates the future.

But after Hall's limitations as a thinker are allowed and perhaps forgiven and his styling and pioneering are acknowledged, a final word must be said about the experiences he provides for the modern reader; for if Hall opened no new worlds to his contemporaries, he may still open one to moderns. In his satires, for example, is a brilliant unfolding of the Elizabethan scene, an access to what his contemporaries found funny, wrongheaded, or disgusting. From them we learn what is persistent in human nature, what subject to fashion. Hall's prose writings provide another sort of pleasure and instruction. Hall's severe moral code perhaps no longer interests us except by contrast. In his world view, however, there is that which is both charming and enviable: a sense of coherence, of order. From Hall we may learn something about an older habit of thought, about the feel of life in an age when each thing seen teaches lessons in wisdom and piety because each thing is a part of a divine creation and a network of clues to the moral life. This is the great unarticulated premise of his work. Even in his generation that coherence was dissipating, as John Donne had cause to lament. But for Hall God's providence, the world's order, and life's meaningfulness were living and eternal truths to which his works as satirist and moralist are enduring monuments.

Notes and References

Chapter One

1. John Marston, *The Scourge of Villanie* (London, 1598), iii, sigs. C8ʳ -D2ʳ.

2. *Observations of Some Specialities of Divine Providence* in *Works of the Right Reverend Joseph Hall, D. D.*, ed. Philip Wynter (Oxford, 1863), I, xx. This autobiographical memoir, along with another, *Hard Measure*, recounting Hall's trials and tribulations during the early years of the Civil War, was written in 1647 and published posthumously in *The Shaking of the Olive Tree* (London, 1660). For more detailed treatments of Hall's life, see biographies by John Jones (1826) and George Lewis (1886).

3. Henry Hastings, third earl of Huntingdon, was named Lord Lieutenant of Leicestershire and Rutlandshire in 1573 and was afterward Lord President of the North. Allied to the House of York on both his mother's and father's side, he was considered a major candidate for the royal succession by Protestant nobles. He died without issue in 1595. See *Dictionary of National Biography*, XXIV, pp. 126–8.

4. *Works*, I, xix.

5. For the curriculum of the Elizabethan grammar school, see T. W. Baldwin, *William Shakespeare's Small Latine & Less Greeke* (Illinois, 1944). The curriculum of the neighboring school at Leicester during Hall's youth is described in W. G. Hoskins, *Provincial England: Essays in Social and Economic History* (London, 1963), p. 102.

6. For Puritan attitudes and doctrine, see William Haller, *The Rise of Puritanism* (Columbia, 1938).

7. A. L. Rowse, *The England of Elizabeth* (New York, 1962), p. 21.

8. Haller, p. 20. See also Tom Fleming Kinlock, *The Life and Works of Joseph Hall, 1574–1656* (London, 1951), pp. 16–7.

9. Of his lectureship, Hall wrote in his *Observations*, "I was encouraged with a sufficient frequence of auditors: but finding that well-applauded work somewhat out of my way, not without a secret blame of myself for so much excursion, I fairly gave up that task, in the midst of those poor acclamations, to a worthy successor, Mr. Dr. Dod and betook myself to those serious

studies which might fit me for that high calling whereunto I was destined."
Works I, xxvi. Thomas Fuller records that Hall "passed all his degrees with
great applause" and was "first noted in the university for his ingenious
maintaining (be it truth or paradox) that *mundus senescit* (the world groweth
old)." *The Worthies of England*, ed. John Freeman (London, 1952), p. 319.

10. Hall refers to these poems in his *Kings Prophecie*, composed on the
accession of James I in 1603. Hall also wrote funeral verses on the death of
William Whitaker in 1596.

11. *The Collected Poems of Joseph Hall* (Liverpool, 1949), xviii.

12. *Works, I*, xxvii.

13. For Hall's relations with the Drurys, see R. C. Bald, *Donne & the
Drurys* (Cambridge, 1959), pp. 50–3, 61–4.

14. *Collected Poems*. All quotations from Hall's poetry are to Davenport's edition.

15. Hall married Elizabeth Winiffe of Brettenham, Suffolk, by whom he
had six sons and two daughters. Of his sons, four followed their father into
the priesthood. The eldest, Robert (1605–1667), became canon of Exeter in
1629 and archdeacon of Cornwall in 1633. Joseph (1607–1669), the second
son, was register of Exeter Cathedral; while the third, George (1612–1668),
became Bishop of Chester and the fourth, Samuel (1616–1674), subdeacon
of Exeter. Elizabeth Hall died 27 August 1652.

16. R. C. Bald, *John Donne: a Life* (Oxford, 1970), pp. 243–4.

17. For the details of the dispute, see Florence S. Teager, "Patronage of
Joseph Hall and John Donne," *Philological Quarterly*, 15 (1936), 408–13.

18. See, for example, David Masson, *Life of Milton* (Cambridge and
London, 1894), II, 213–68 and 356–409.

19. *Works*, I, lxviii.

20. Hall desired to be buried outside the church building rather than in
the nave, as was customary, but his wish was not followed. A transcript of
Bishop Hall's will may be found in *Works*, I, lxxvii-lxxxi.

21. *Worthies of England*, p. 320.

22. The importance of Humanism in the Renaissance has become a
commonplace of modern scholarship. See C. S. Lewis, *English Literature in
the Sixteenth Century, Excluding Drama* (Oxford, 1954), pp. 18–32 for a
useful corrective to the idea that the Humanists were the intellectual heroes
of their time and R. Weiss, *Humanism in England During the Fifteenth
Century*, 2nd ed. (Blackwell, 1957), p. 1 for a succinct definition of
"Humanist": " . . . the scholar who studied the writings of ancient authors
without fear of supernatural anticiceronian warnings, searched for manu-
scripts of lost or rare classical texts, collected the works of classical writers,
and attempted to learn Greek and write like the ancient authors of Rome."

23. Hall's theory of imitation is discussed in Harold Ogden White,
Plagiarism and Imitation During the English Renaissance (Harvard, 1935),
pp. 120–4. The *Oxford English Dictionary* credits Hall with the first re-

corded use of the word plagiarism ("plagiary") in *Virgidemiarum* (1598).

24. Quintilian, after Cicero the most influential of classical rhetoricians in the Renaissance, had observed, "It is a universal rule of life that we should wish to copy what we approve in others." *Institutio Oratoria*, trans. H. E. Butler (Harvard, 1958), X, ii.

Chapter Two

1. Mary Claire Randolph, "The Medical Concept in English Renaissance Satiric Theory: its Possible Relationships and Implications," *Studies in Philology*, 38 (1941), 125–57.

2. *Elizabethan Poetry* (Harvard, 1952), p. 194.

3. Bound with Hall's "three books" were a verse tragedy, *Simond*, and two other poems by author or authors unknown.

4. The genitive *virgidemiarum* is governed by the English words, "three books." I follow the common practice of using the nominative *virgidemiae* when referring to the satires. Davenport finds precedent for Hall's use of this rare word in Varro's *Saturae Menippeae*, III, 3 and in Plautus, *Rudens*, III, ii, 22. *Collected Poems of Joseph Hall*, p. 159

5. *The Cankered Muse. Satire of the English Renaissance* (Yale, 1959), pp. 7–8. Kernan's is the fullest study of satiric conventions in the English Renaissance. But see also Arnold Stein, "Donne's Obscurity and the Elizabethan Tradition," *English Literary History*, 13 (1946), 98–118 and Mary Claire Randolph, "The Structural Design of Formal Verse Satire," *Philological Quarterly*, 21 (1942), 368–84.

6. Milton wrote, "That such a poem should be toothless I still affirm it to be a bull, taking away the essence of that which it calls itself. For if it bite neither the persons nor the vices, how is it a satire, and if it bite either, how is it toothless, so that toothless satires are as much as if he had said toothless teeth." *An Apology Against a Pamphlet Call'd a Modest Confutation* in *Works*, ed. Frank Allen Patterson *et al* (Columbia, 1931), III (part 1), 329.

7. In his Post-Script Hall wrote, "I think my first satire doth somewhat resemble the sour and crabbed face of Juvenal." On the originality of Hall's "imitation" see Arnold Davenport, "Interfused Sources in Joseph Hall's Satires," *Review of English Studies*, 18 (1942), 208–213, and Arnold Stein, "Joseph Hall's Imitation of Juvenal," *Modern Language Review*, 43 (1948), 315–22.

8. *English Literature in the Sixteenth Century* (Oxford, 1954), p. 471. Lewis is hard on Hall, finding him "in constant danger of relapsing into flat querulousness." But he also finds good words for Hall's "advertisement for a Chaplain" (II. vi), observing that "Nashe, or even Donne, would have spoiled it by exaggeration and made the advertiser a monster."

9. Pope, according to Nichol's *Anecdotes* (V, 654), presented a copy of the 1599 edition of *Virgidemiae* to a Mr. West, remarking that "he es-

teemed them the best poetry and truest satire in the English language, and that he had the intention of modernizing them, as he had done some of Dr. Donne's."

10. As Arnold Stein observes, Marston was probably more indebted to Hall for his satiric manner and matter than he was to Juvenal. See Stein, "The Second English Satirist," *Modern Language Review*, 38 (1943), 273–78.

11. Healey's translation has been edited by Huntington Brown (Harvard, 1937), and, except for a short selection from *liber* 1 in *Ideal Commonwealths*, ed. Henry Morley (London, 1887), it is the only English version.

12. For arguments against Hall's authorship, however, see Edward A. Petherick, "On the Authorship of *Mundus Alter et Idem*," *Gentleman's Magazine*, 281 (July, 1896), 66–73.

13. *Works*, III (Part I), 294–5.

14. See Sanford M. Salyer, "Renaissance Influences in Hall's *Mundus Alter et Idem*," *Philological Quarterly*, 6 (1927), 321–34. Huntington Brown identified Lucian's *True History* as the prototype of Hall's satire. Both satires are first-person narrations of fantastic voyages to Antipodean regions; and both authors are given to invented place names that echo real ones, have a knack for verisimilitude while in the midst of bald-faced lying, and a penchant for ridiculing contemporary fashions in philosophy and religion. The very name of Hall's narrator recalls Lucian's frequent use of Hermes, or Mercury, as a character in his *Dialogues*. *Discovery of a New World*, p. xxvi.

15. For this topic, see Ernst Robert Curtius, *European Literature and the Latin Middle Ages*, trans. Williard R. Trask (New York, 1953), pp. 94–8.

Chapter Three

1. The influence of Ramism—the doctrine of the French academic Peter Ramus (Pierre de la Ramée)—can be detected in the structure of Hall's treatise as outlined in its "Analysis of Resolution," a one-page diagram opposite the dedicatory preface. Like Ramists in general, Hall proceeds to analyze his subject by constant subdivision. For Ramist dichotomies and the influence of Ramism in England, especially at Hall's Cambridge, see Wilber Samuel Howell, *Logic and Rhetoric in England, 1500–1700* (Princeton, 1956), pp. 146–281, and W. J. Ong, *Ramus: Method, and the Decay of Dialogue* (Harvard, 1958), esp. pp. 199–202.

2. "What we are seeking, therefore," Seneca explains, "is how the mind may always pursue a steady and favourable course, may be well-disposed towards itself, and may view its condition with joy, and suffer no interruption of this joy, but may abide in a peaceful state, being never uplifted nor ever cast down. This will be 'Tranquillity'." *Moral Essays*, trans. John W. Basore (Harvard, 1958), II, 215.

3. L. D. Reynolds, *The Medieval Tradition of Seneca's Letters* (Oxford, 1965), pp. 112–24.

4. For a discussion of Seneca's influence on English ethical thought, see Herschel Baker, *The Wars of Truth* (Harvard, 1952), pp. 110–6; Ralph Graham Palmer, *Seneca's De Remediis Fortuitorum and the Elizabethans* (Chicago, 1953), pp. 1–25; and Basil Willey, *The English Moralists* (New York, 1964), pp. 66–90.

5. For discussions of Hall's "Senecanism" or "Neostoicism," see Joseph Hall, *Heaven Upon Earth and Characters of Vertues and Vices*, ed. Rudolph Kirk (Rutgers, 1948), pp. 19–51; Philip A. Smith, "Bishop Hall, 'Our English Seneca,'" *Publications of the Modern Language Association*, 63 (1948), 1191–1204; and Audrey Chew, "Joseph Hall and Neo-Stoicism," *Publications of the Modern Language Association*, 65 (1950), 1130–45. Kirk and Smith see Hall as the leading neo-Stoic of the seventeenth century; Chew stresses Hall's essentially medieval attitude toward Seneca, noting that he "went to Seneca not for new ideas but because in Seneca he could find a reinforcement of old ones—ideas that had been current at least all through the sixteenth century" (p. 1133).

6. All quotations from Hall's prose are from *The Works of the Right Reverend Joseph Hall, D.D. Bishop of Exeter and Norwich*, 10 vols. (Oxford, 1863). To reduce the number of footnotes, I cite volume and page in parentheses.

7. Henry W. Sams, "Anti-Stoicism in Seventeenth- and Early Eighteenth-Century England," *Studies in Philology*, 41 (1944), 65–78. According to Sams, Stoicism was criticized by seventeenth-century Englishmen for its apathy, paganism, and belief in the sufficiency of natural reason. Hall condemns each of these views in *Heaven Upon Earth*.

8. *Epistulae Morales*, trans. R. M. Gummere (Harvard, 1953), I, 171.

9. For the background of the English "Character," see Edward Chauncey Baldwin, "The Relation of the English 'Character' to its Greek Prototype," *PMLA*, 18 (1903), 412–23; Wendell Clausen, "The Beginnings of English Character-Writing in the Early Seventeenth Century," *Philological Quarterly*, 25 (1946), 32–45; and Benjamin Boyce, *The Theophrastan Character in England to 1642* (Harvard, 1947), pp. 3–121. As Boyce points out, Hall had written what were in essence characters in his earlier works, *Mundus Alter et Idem*, *Meditations and Vowes* (1606) and *Heaven Upon Earth*.

10. *Elizabethan Critical Essays*, ed. Gregory Smith (London, reprt. 1950), II, 148.

11. On this familiar Renaissance concept, see E. M. W. Tillyard, *The Elizabethan World Picture* (New York, 1944), pp. 87–100.

12. The judgment of Clausen, p. 43, and Baldwin, "Jonson's Indebtedness to the Greek Character-Sketch," *Modern Language Notes*, 16 (1901),

394. Douglas Bush, *English Literature in the Earlier Seventeenth Century 1600–1660*, p. 199, is no more generous, noting that Hall "continually mingles comment and interpretation, so that his vices are not free from abstraction and his verities are almost wholly abstract." For a favorable and thorough evaluation and interpretation, see Gerhard Müller-Schwefe, "Joseph Hall's *Characters of Vertues and Vices:* Notes Toward a Revaluation," *Texas Studies in Literature and Language*, 14 (1972), 235–51.

13. Boyce, pp. 136–7.

14. Müller-Schwefe, pp. 248–51, corrects Kirk's data on Hall's foreign publication.

15. For the relationship of letter writing to rhetoric, see William G. Crane, *Wit and Rhetoric in the Renaissance* (1937; rept. Gloucester, Mass., 1964), pp. 108–112.

16. The inevitability of death was a favorite argument of Seneca in his consolatory epistles (see, *Ad Marciam de consolatione*, X. 6), although Hall hardly had need to report to Seneca for it. A large store of classical and Christian consolatory topoi was available to Renaissance authors; the *consolatione* was a common rhetorical exercise in the schools and universities, and it is therefore impossible to determine the exact origin of Hall's arguments, if such should be deemed necessary. Hall does share Seneca's premise that the more reasons one can provide to dissuade excessive grief the better, although for different motives. To Seneca excessive grief was ridiculous; to Hall it was impious.

17. Tom Fleming Kinloch, *The Life and Works of Joseph Hall, 1574–1656*, p. 145. Kinloch remarks, "Here, as elsewhere in his controversial writings, Hall shows himself to be entirely destitute of imaginative insight and compassion. The Scrooby congregation did not leave England out of mere willfulness . . . . He did not, he could not conceive, that a time was to come when a great nation would regard these humble peasants as heroes . . . "

18. So-called by Thomas Fuller for the "pureness, plainness, and fulness of his style." *Worthies*, p. 320. In a letter from Sir Henry Wotton to Samuel Collins, 17 January 1637, Wotton referred to Hall as our "spiritual Seneca." *Life and Letters of Sir Henry Wotton*, ed. L. P. Smith (Oxford, 1907), II, 370. The sobriquet was apparently not uncommon.

19. *Works*, III (Part I), 321.

20. The beginnings of anti-Ciceronianism have been traced by Morris Croll in a series of essays collected in *Style, Rhetoric, and Rhythm*, ed. J. Max Patrick, Robert O. Evans, *et al.* (Princeton, 1966). Supplementing Croll is George Williamson, *The Senecan Amble* (Chicago, 1951). For a dissenting view of Hall's Senecanism, see Harold Fisch, "The Limits of Hall's Senecanism," *Proceedings of the Leeds Philosophical Society*, 6 (1950), 453–63.

21. *Works*, ed. Basil Montagu (Philadelphia, 1876), I, 170.

22. Croll, pp. 54–64.

23. On this aspect of Ramism, see Perry Miller, *The New Englar.d Mind: the Seventeenth-Century* (Harvard, 1954), pp. 300–62, and W. J. Ong, pp. 212–13 and 283–88.

24. Croll, pp. 176, 192.

Chapter Four

1. On the conventions of the Renaissance funeral elegy, see A. L. Bennett, "The Principal Rhetorical Conventions in the Renaissance Personal Elegy," *Studies in Philology*, 51 (1954), 107–26 and O. B. Hardison, *The Enduring Monument* (Chapel Hill, 1962), pp. 107–62.

2. *Collected Poems of Joseph Hall*, p. 265.

3. See Leonard D. Tourney, "Convention and Wit in Donne's *Elegie* on Prince Henry," *Studies in Philology*, 71 (1974), pp. 473–83.

4. *Poems*, ed. Herbert J. C. Grierson (Oxford, 1912), I, p. 203.

5. R. C. Bald, *Donne and the Drurys*, pp. 69–84 and Bald, *John Donne: A Life*, p. 274.

6. *Conversations with Drummond of Hathornden* in *Ben Jonson*, ed. C. H. Herford and Percy Simpson (Oxford, 1925), I., p. 136.

7. For discussions of the prefaces as criticism, see Leonard D. Tourney, "Joseph Hall and the *Anniversaries*," *Papers on Language & Literature*, 13 (1977), 25–34; Barbara K. Lewalski, *Donne's Anniversaries and the Poetry of Praise* (Princeton, 1973), pp. 220–25; and Hardison, *The Enduring Monument*, pp. 163–6.

8. See Lily B. Campbell, *Divine Poetry and Drama in Sixteenth-Century England* (Cambridge, 1961), pp. 34–54.

9. The effect of the Psalms on George Herbert, for example, has been studied by Coburn Freer, *Music for a King: George Herbert's Style and the Metrical Psalms* (Baltimore and London, 1972). The classic essay on the general subject of psalmody and prosody is that of Hallet Smith, "English Metrical Psalms in the Sixteenth Century and Their Literary Significance," *Huntington Library Quarterly*, 9 (1946), 249–70.

10. *The First and Second Prayer Books of Edward VI* (London, 1949), p. 32.

11. *Poems of Sir Philip Sidney*, ed. William A. Ringer (Oxford, 1962), p. 270. I have modernized spelling.

Chapter Five

1. *Poems*, I, 157. I have modernized spelling.

2. *English Literature in the Early Seventeenth Century*, p. 294. On the variety and popularity of devotional works, see Louis B. Wright, *Middle-Class Culture in Elizabethan England* (North Carolina, 1935), pp. 228–96, and Helen C. White, *English Devotional Literature, 1600–1640* (Wisconsin, 1930), passim.

3. See, for example, Louis L. Martz, *The Poetry of Meditation* (Yale, 1954), esp. pp. 1–22, 67–70, and 331–52.

4. Apparently by oversight, the third "century" of *Meditations and Vowes* contains 101 meditations.

5. For traditional rhetorical devices of expansion and their use in Renaissance prose, see Crane, *Wit and Rhetoric in the Renaissance*, chs. 4 and 5.

6. Stanley E. Fish, *Self-Consuming Artifacts* (California, 1972), chap. 2.

7. Martz has identified Hall's monk as Joannes Mauburnus, whose *Rosetum*, a treatise on meditation, appeared anonymously in Basle in 1504 and in Paris in 1510; and Martz also compares Hall's "Scale of Meditation" with Mauburnus' to show indebtedness. *Poetry of Meditation*, pp. 331–7. Frank L. Huntley argues, however, that the monk is Thomas à Kempis, author of *De Imitatione Christi*, "Bishop Hall and Protestant Meditation," *Studies in the Literary Imagination*, X (1977), 62.

8. See Martz, pp. 6–10, and White, pp. 68 and 109.

9. *Spiritual Exercises of St. Ignatius*, ed. C. Lattey (London, 1928), p. 2.

10. Huntley, pp. 59–60.

11. *Life and Works*, p. 61.

12. Hall's influence on later writers of meditations is discussed by Elbert N. S. Thompson, *The Seventeenth-Century English Essay* (Iowa, 1926), pp. 66–85 and Harold Fisch, "Bishop Hall's Meditations," *Review of English Studies*, 25 (1949), pp. 219–21. See also, H. H. Erskine-Hill, "Edmund Waller and Samuel Butler: Two Poetic Debts to Hall's *Occasional Meditations*," *Notes and Queries, New Series*, 12 (1965), 133–4.

13. Extracts from Whitefoot's sermon may be found in Hall's *Works*, I, lxxii–lxxvii.

14. Quoted by Fisch, p. 220.

Chapter Six

1. *Works*, I, xxxvi. Hall was meticulous in preparation: "yet never durst I climb into the pulpit to preach any sermon, whereof I had not before in my poor and plain fashion penned every word, in the same order wherein I hoped to deliver it, although in the expression I listed not to be a slave to syllables."

2. See Alan Fager Herr, *The Elizabethan Sermon: a Survey and a Bibliography* (1940; rpt. New York, 1969), pp. 119–69. Herr's bibliography lists all the Elizabethan sermons recorded in the *Short Title Catalogue* and then some 513 separate publications including about 1200 sermons. See also W. Fraser Mitchell, *English Pulpit Oratory from Andrewes to Tillotston* (1932; rpt. New York, 1962), pp. 411–452. Mitchell's book, the standard work on the seventeenth-century sermon, contains a select bibliography of representative sermons.

3. *English Literature in the Earlier Seventeenth Century*, p. 296.

4. On the relationship of rhetoric and the sermons see Mitchell, pp. 93–130.

5. The controversy of sermon styles between Puritan and Anglicans is ably set forth by Perry Miller, *The New England Mind: the Seventeenth-Century*, pp. 331–62.

6. On the limitations of Donne's scholarship, see, for example, Don Cameron Allen, "Dean Donne Sets his Text," *English Literary History*, 10 (1943), 208–220.

7. Mitchell observes that Hall's sermon style "more nearly resembles the Restoration manner of preaching, before the reform movement of the Royal Society preachers had banished both allusion and quotation, than that of any other Jacobean preacher." P. 225.

Chapter Seven

1. See W. K. Jordan, *The Development of Religious Toleration in England* (1932: rpt. Gloucester, Mass., 1965) pp. 34–43. According to Horton Davies, the great Anglican apologists of the Elizabethan period—Whitgift, Bancroft, and Hooker—"produced an armoury against the slings and arrows of Puritanism." *Worship and Theology in England* (Princeton, 1960), I, p. 40. For the attitude of English Protestants toward Roman Catholicism, see Charles H. George and Katherine George, *The Protestant Mind of the English Reformation 1570–1640* (Princeton, 1961), pp. 375–97.

2. On the soundness of Hall's argument, see George, p. 376. "The Protestant drive toward the multiplying of creeds and churches has been so obvious, in fact, and so often pointed to and commented upon that it has been in a real sense over-emphasized. Partly in consequence, the types and degrees of difference within Roman Catholicism have been insufficiently acknowledged and allowed to conceal themselves too completely behind the massive bulk of an institutional unity."

3. Hall's were the general views of Protestants. See George and George, pp. 265–275. Hooker also believed single life "more angelical and divine": *Ecclesiastical Polity*, (Dent, 1968), II, p. 391.

4. Foremost among Hall's attackers was Henry Burton (1578–1648), Puritan rector of St. Matthews Church, London, and a zealous hater of bishops. For a full discussion of his quarrel with Hall, see Rudolph Kirk, "A Seventeenth Century Controversy: Extremism vs. Moderation," *Texas Studies in Literature and Language*, 9 (1967), 5–35.

5. In his *Laws of Ecclesiastical Polity* (1593–1600), Hooker defined the theology and government of the Church of England for generations to come. Not merely a polemic but a major philosophical work, Hooker's *Laws* undertook to explain the nature of law and man and to defend the place of human reason in God's economy. Hooker held that scripture was not the sole authority for church government. Human reason, a gift of God, might

also dictate civil and ecclesiastical laws and might sustain or institute ordinances as circumstances direct. But because what men have long believed and practiced is likely to be reasonable, institution and doctrines should not be changed capriciously; even if the scriptural authority of a practice or institution is questioned, its usefulness may still be affirmed if it conforms to the light of reason. Thus, the Roman Catholics err in their obeisance to tradition, the Puritans in their demand for scriptural warrant. The *via media* looks both to scripture and to tradition in the light of reason, holding neither as sole authority.

6. On Hall's superiority as scholar and rhetorician to the Smectymnuans, see William Riley Parker, *Milton: a Biography* (Oxford, 1968), I, pp. 205–6.

7. The moral and religious values they shared are discussed by Audrey Chew, "Joseph Hall and John Milton," *English Literary History*, 17 (1950), 274–84.

Chapter Eight

1. *Allegory of Love* (Oxford, 1936), pp. 158–9.
2. *English Literature in the Early Seventeenth Century*, p. 199n.

Selected Bibliography

PRIMARY SOURCES

1. Complete works
HALL, JOSEPH. *The Works of Joseph Hall.* 10 vols. Ed. Josiah Pratt. London: Williams and Smith, 1808.
———. *The Works of Joseph Hall.* 12 vols. Ed. Peter Hall. Oxford: D.A. Talboys, 1837–39.
———. *Works of the Right Reverend Joseph Hall, D.D.* 10 vols. Ed. Philip Wynter. Oxford: Oxford University Press, 1863. Standard edition available in facsimile reprint by AMS Press, Inc. New York, 1969.

2. Poetry
The Complete Poems of Joseph Hall. Ed. A.B. Grosart. Manchester: C.E. Sims, 1879.
The Collected Poems of Joseph Hall. Ed. Arnold Davenport. Liverpool: University of Liverpool Press, 1949.

3. Prose
Heaven Upon Earth and Characters of Vertues and Vices. Ed. Rudolph Kirk. New Brunswick: Rutgers University Press, 1948. Contains useful introductory essays on the literary form of characters, Hall's neo-Stoic thought, and influence on the Continent.
The Discovery of a New World (Mundus Alter et Idem). Ed. Huntington Brown. Cambridge: Harvard University Press, 1937. Contains an excellent critical essay on Hall's satire.

SECONDARY SOURCES

1. Biographies
JONES, JOHN. *Bishop Hall, His Life and Times.* London: L. B. Seeley, 1826. Early biography, based largely on Hall's own memoirs and works. Takes little interest in Hall as man of letters.
KINLOCK, TOM FLEMING. *The Life and Works of Joseph Hall, 1574–1656.*

London: Staples Press, 1951. Includes some analysis of Hall's work, although weakened by Kinlock's evident dislike for Hall.

LEWIS, GEORGE. *A Life of Joseph Hall, D.D.* London: Hodder and Stoughton, 1886. The best biography, contains information lacking in Jones.

2. Criticism

BOYCE, BENJAMIN. *The Theophrastan Character in England to 1642.* Cambridge: Harvard University Press, 1947. Describes the tradition of character writing in which Hall worked.

CHEW, AUDREY. "Joseph Hall and John Milton." *Journal of English Literary History,* 17 (1950), 274–95. Discusses the views of Hall and Milton on church government and personal morals.

————. "Joseph Hall and Neo-Stocism." *PMLA,* 65 (1950), 1130–45. Questions Hall's preeminence as leading neo-Stoic of the seventeenth century, finding him rather conservatively adapting Stoic teachings to Christian use.

DAVENPORT, ARNOLD. "Interfused Sources in Joseph Hall's Satires." *Review of English Studies,* 18 (1942), 208–13. Argues for Hall's creative adaptation of Roman models in composing his satires.

FISCH, HAROLD. "Bishop Hall's Meditations." *Review of English Studies,* 25 (1949), 210–21. An excellent discussion of the thought and style of Hall's meditations.

————. "The Limits of Hall's Senecanism." *Proceedings of the Leeds Philosophical Society,* 6 (1950), 453–63. Finds Hall both selective in his use of Senecan thought and obedience to the norms of Senecan style.

HUNTLEY, FRANK L. "Bishop Hall and Protestant Meditation." *Studies in the Literary Imagination,* X (1977), 57–71. Relates Hall's meditative practice to the background of Protestant and Catholic systems.

JENSEN, EJNER J. "Hall and Marston: the Role of the Satirist." *Satire Newsletter,* 4 (1967), 72–83. A useful discussion of Hall's satiric technique, concluding that Hall is superior to Marston in versification and satiric strategy.

KAUFMANN, U. MILO. *The Pilgrim's Progress and Traditions in Puritan Meditation.* New Haven and London: Yale University Press, 1966. Finds Hall a major influence in Puritan meditation in the seventeenth century.

KERNAN, ALVIN. *The Cankered Muse: Satire of the English Renaissance.* New Haven: Yale University Press, 1959. Studies conventions and themes of English satire in the sixteenth century.

KIRK, RUDOLF. "A Seventeenth-Century Controversy: Extremism vs. Moderation." *Texas Studies in Literature and Language,* 9 (1967), 5–35. A detailed account of Hall's controversy with Henry Burton and other Puritans over the status of the Roman Church.

MITCHELL, W. FRASER. *English Pulpit Oratory From Andrewes to Tillot-son.* New York: Russell & Russell, 1962. The standard work on sermon styles in the seventeenth century.

MÜLLER-SCHWEFE, GERHARD. "Joseph Hall's *Characters of Vertues and Vices:* Notes Toward a Revaluation." *Texas Studies in Literature and Language,* 14 (1972), 235–51. A positive reassessment of Hall's *Characters* and useful list of translations of Hall's works in French and German.

SALYER, SANFORD M. "Renaissance Influences in Hall's *Mundus Alter et Idem.*" *Philological Quarterly,* 6 (1927), 321–34. Finds evidence for Hall's widespread reading and debt to Renaissance authors. Along with Huntington Brown's introduction (see above), the most thorough examination of Hall's Latin prose satire.

SMITH, PHILIP A. "Bishop Hall, 'Our English Seneca.' " *PMLA,* 63 (1948), 1191–1204. Argues, somewhat superficially, that Hall is the leading neo-Stoic of the seventeenth century.

STEIN, ARNOLD. "Joseph Hall's Imitation of Juvenal." *Modern Language Review,* 43 (1948), 315–22. Affirms Hall's independence as an artist by showing how he made creative use of his classical models.

TOURNEY, LEONARD D. "Joseph Hall and the *Anniversaries.*" *Papers on Language & Literature,* 13 (1977), 25–34. Evaluates Hall's performance as literary critic in his two prefatory poems to Donne's *Anniversaries.*

WILLIAMSON, GEORGE. *The Senecan Amble.* Chicago: University of Chicago Press, 1951. An exhaustively thorough examination of the various prose styles labelled "Senecan" in the seventeenth century; useful, if intermittent, references to Hall help to place him in context.

Index